Thom Dekles
"Bassist"

Michael Adou

Thanks for yo
love + support.

Janay S. Madison

D1203374

Matthew R_____
LOVE YA

Bam
Bam
Much LOVE

_____ R Holmes
PEACE

Bryant McClurkin
(Zister) BOSS

A Bridge To Success

"ONE MAN'S VISION CHANGED THE LIVES OF MANY"

By Charles Lott Miller (a.k.a. Chuck Miller)

ISBN 978-0-557-92665-7

Other Products Co-written and or written and performed by Charles L. Miller

A book in titled: AFRICAN AMERICAN JAZZ and RAP
"Social and Philosophical Examination of Black Expressive Behavior"
Edited by James L. Conyers, Jr.

A Jazz CD in titled: Changes for Tena

Ask for them at your local bookstores/CD music stores; visit CDbaby on the internet or on the
web: www.sealottmusic.com

Scripture quotations marked *TLB* are taken from the *Holy Bible*, The Living Bible *Version* of the Bible, Copyright 1971 by Tyndale House Publishers. Used by permission.

Grateful acknowledgement is made to the late Calvin Howell, Greg Lawson, Bryan Fisher, Eddie Grant, and Gary Williams for use of their telephone interviews. Used by permission.

Special thanks to UNO Yearbook, The Omaha Star, The Omaha World Herald, The Metro News, The Air Pulse and The Gateway News paper for use of photos and quotations.

Except where otherwise indicated, all photos are courtesy of the private collection of Chuck Miller.

ACKNOWLEDGEMENTS

To my wife Chestene (a.k.a. Tena)

I am grateful for her love, her trust and her belief in me. She has lived most of her life helping me to become the man, the father and the musician I have become. She is everything I have ever wanted in a faithful wife. May God continue to bless her throughout her life.

Charles L. (a.k.a. Chuck) Miller

ENDORSEMENT

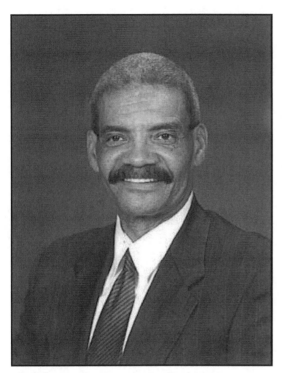

Photo courtesy of Reverend Darryl C. Eure

Omaha? Omaha? Omaha? Who haven't heard of it? No it's not in another country. No it's not a lost planet in the universe. You remember D-Day when the allied forces came on shore in what was known as Omaha Beach during World War II.? Well that's not the Omaha I'm writing about. Omaha? Come on and think. Omaha... Is it an Indian Tribe? Well yea, but there is something else about Omaha. I remember now something about animals? Yea; there is something about wild animals; Mutual of Omaha, and Wild Kingdom? Now you're getting real close. Omaha isn't a name that you hear every day on the news, in history or in the area of entertainment. Most people on the west coast think that we are all farmers that are in bed when the sun goes down. There is life in Omaha!

Omaha is a city located in the heart of the United States. Fact, we are not a big city, nor are we a small city, we are not a cow town in the middle of cornstalks. Omaha is a medium size city with believe it or not a sizeable African American population. We don't compare in size or culture to New York

City, Chicago, or Los Angeles but you know, when I was coming of age during the 1950's, 60's and 70's, we Omahans always thought we were the big little city on the banks of the Missouri River with a big city style.

Omaha is the little big city that produced the following icons: movie and television stars, Marlin Brando, Henry Fonda, and Johnny Carson; football great Gale Sayers, Marlin Briscoe and Ahman Green; pro basketball players Bob Boozer and Ron Boone; baseball great Bob Gibson, and Heisman trophy winners, Johnny Rogers and Eric Croche. Omaha is where Whitney M. Young got his start as National Director of the Urban League. Omaha is the birth place of former President Gerald Ford, and political activist Malcolm X. Even today, Omaha is still rich in history and culture. Omaha is the home of Warren Buffet, one of the wealthiest persons in the world. We still have one of the most outspoken and respected civil rights activist in this country living right here in Omaha, former State Senator, Ernie Chambers.

I have often been asked why I love Omaha so much. It's not so much my love for Omaha as it is for my love for North Omaha. Back in the day, the white people used to call North Omaha the near north side. That was their way of identifying the black part of town. Well, I can only tell you that in my time, North Omaha was the Mecca for black people. We grew up in a time when black people migrated to Omaha from the south looking to find a better life for themselves and their families. If you were willing to work hard you could find a job at one of several packing housing in the city, or you could work for the railroad, or at one of the many hotels downtown. Money wasn't too bad for a hardworking black family. You could live in a house that was your own, in a neighborhood where everyone knew everyone else. You could live in a community where you could raise your children. My father came here in the 1940's from New York City. He was in the army stationed in Hastings, Nebraska. He grew up on the streets of Harlem. He use to tell us stories about how he loved to go to the night spots in Harlem to see the likes of Nat King Cole, Count Basie, Lionel

Hampton, Billie Holiday, Cab Calloway, and other black music greats. While in the Army, my father would travel to Omaha on the weekends and party at the USO Club where he met and married my mother. My brothers and I use to ask my father why he and my mother never moved back to New York City. He said; because Omaha had everything Harlem had in New York. He also said; North Omaha was like a smaller Harlem, but without all of the traffic.

Most of the black folks in North Omaha lived for the weekends which started on Thursday night. Most of the packing housing and railroads paid their workers on Thursday or Friday. So the bars and hotspots around North Omaha started getting into the groove on Thursday night. The men with their long cars, pinned stripped suits and the beautiful women with their hair styled, dressed in fine clothes hit the streets to find music and dancing.

North Omaha was noted for a three miles street known as (the duce) or 24th Street. Great jazz flowed from the doors of the Dreamland Ballroom, Allen Showcase, The Off Beat, and The Elks Club. On many occasions when professional groups were hired to perform at large theatres downtown for white audiences, who by the way paid large sums of money to see and hear them perform; after their performances, you might see these groups performing free and eating at one of the local North Omaha establishments. Count Basie, Nat Cole, Earl "Fatha" Hines, Dizzy Gillespie, Duke Ellington, and Cab Calloway are a few groups that blessed our hearts with this great music.

North Omaha had its own talented jazz musicians which included the great Preston Love who performed with the Count Basie Orchestra throughout the world and Basie Givens and His Orchestra. Not only did we have Preston Love, we also had Buddy Miles, Andrea Lewis, Ronnie and Donnie Beck, Calvin Keys and then there was my friend and brother in Christ, Professor Charles L. Miller (a.k.a. Chuck Miller).

During the latter part of the 1950's into the 1960's and 1970's my brother Harry and I were entertainers. We performed on stages throughout Omaha as tap dancers; we patented ourselves after the Nicholas Brothers. Usually we performed before the vocal singers and bands came out to do their performances. One of the performers in the band was a young trumpet player who played like a seasoned professional. That young man was Chuck Miller. I would always hang around the stage area to hear Chuck Miller play. He and his instrument were one in the same. He blended the melody into a beautiful sound that made the audience become silent and later roar with applause after his solos.

I couldn't play an instrument, but because I grew up listening to great jazz performers on hundreds of records my father would play, I developed an ear for good music. I knew good music when I heard it and Chuck Miller had it; it was as Quincy Jones would say, "in the pocket." Each time I heard Chuck play I knew that he wasn't just some instrumentalist joining onto a band to get a little neighborhood fame, he was for real. He was a professional jazz musician, a teacher and a leader.

As a young man I would travel to night clubs just to hear Chuck play. Some instrumentalists would play for the audience; they knew what notes to hit to get a roar from the audience. However, Chuck Miller played the complete music. When he played, he was in a world of his own. Through his trumpet he would invite everyone into his world. Chuck's world was deep, soulful and spiritual. My father and I would sit in the dimly lit club and listen intently as Chuck played and my father would say, "now that's jazz!" Everyone can't play jazz. What some called jazz today isn't real jazz; it feels good, but it has no real soul. It sounds good, but so does elevator music. Jazz is a sound that enters deep into your soul. When a jazz musician is "in the pocket", your soul is satisfied. It's like being at church. Chuck Miller has been blessed by God with a special gift; a gift that he shares with everyone.

Chuck has developed a way to teach people with little or no knowledge of music how to read musical notes and how to make those written notes come alive on their instrument. Chuck Miller has developed a music theory that is holistic. By this

I mean Chuck helps develops the musical talents, and use music as a way of motivating youth who are at-risk to develop self-esteem and respect for themselves and a healthy outlook for their community. This holistic approach of music instruction takes at-risk youths off the streets and gives them a medium in which they can express themselves through music.

Chuck Miller is passionate about helping others develop the best in themselves. That is why he is sought by children and adults as a teacher. Chuck has provided instructions to literally hundreds of young people throughout the world. He has helped many of them form choirs, bands, big bands and encouraged shy instrumentalists to use their God given talents.

Throughout this book you will discover how during the 1970's and throughout the 1980's at the North Omaha Gene Eppley Boys Club, Chuck took the raw unused talents of at-risk children and developed them into singers and performers in rock/jazz bands, R&B/jazz bands and big bands. Many of the children taught by Chuck Miller have grown up into productive musicians and have become professional with their craft.

In 2005 Chuck Miller was inducted into the Omaha *Black Music Hall of Fame*. He has received countless awards and recognition for his great work with young people. He would be the first to say that with all the recognition he has received and all of the music success he has enjoyed, he could not have accomplished all that he has without the loving support of his family. It can truly be said: "to the side of every good man there is a good woman." That woman is Chestene Miller who is the life long love of his life. The life of a teacher, musician and entertainer is not always easy. There are many times when the master musician had to be away from home traveling from city to city. Keeping the home fire burning was Chestene Miller who in reality is a God fearing and gracious woman!

There is a passage in the Bible from the book of Revelation 14:13 which say: "Blessed are the dead who die in the Lord from henceforth: Yea, saith the Spirit that they may rest from their labors; and their works do follow them."

As a Pastor, I have talked to people who asked, "Why can't we live forever?" Well, we can through our good works. The labor (the good works) of Chuck Miller will let him live forever. For long after the earthly life of Chuck Miller is over, he will continue to live on through the hundreds of children he has worked with at The Gene Eppley North Omaha Boys Club throughout the city of Omaha. God has blessed him to influence musicians from around the country and the world.

May God continue to bless Chuck and the great work he has done that has saved so many at-risk youth and allowed them to develop their own special gifts from God. This book he has written will become a Mecca of history and love for the Omaha community. Because of the positive motivation given to our young people by the teaching and musicianship of Chuck Miller, our young people of the past, present and the future can truly say, "*Our lives have truly changed!*"

----Reverend Darryl C. Eure
Pastor/Freestone Baptist Church

Table of Contents

PREFACE

"To everyone who is victorious, I will give fruit from the Tree of Life in the Paradise of God." Revelation 2:7b, The Living Bible Version[i].

To receive love, joy, peace, patience, kindness, goodness, faithfulness, gentleness and self-control from others is a dream we all share. *These are The Fruit of the Spirit, Galatians 5:22-23, The Living Bible Version*[ii].

Everyone wants to be loved and respected especially by his or her immediate family. This was not always possible in the lives of many of our African American youth in Omaha, Nebraska during the 1970's and even today. There were many during this time that suffered greatly from the lost of a father or a mother to the Criminal Justice System and to drugs.

Many single parents struggled to raise their children in a home unfilled with *The Fruit of the Spirit*; the weight was just too heavy. As a result and in desperation, many turned to The North Omaha Boys Club (later called The Club) for support. The Club offered a new ray of hope and gave the community a way out of this vicious circle of life.

This book tells the story of a young college music student who takes on the challenge of enriching the lives of eight at-risk young men, a young lady and later a generation of others.

Armed with the desire of helping others by using music performance and music education, as motivation, and training them at The North Omaha Boys Club, new generations of local professionals were born.

This task was accomplished by looking at the complete child and all the factors that potentially affected their future. This book however, will concentrate on one factor, music. Bands were very popular during this time and we used this vehicle to develop Positive Self-Images and Self-Esteem in the children of Omaha, Nebraska.

This story is more than kids playing in a band. This is the lesson that a group of at-risk youth from the inner city of Omaha learned from a most experienced teacher/musician.

These were youngsters who were set on becoming professional musicians and nothing; nothing, nothing in the world was going to stop them. They even went as far as breaking into a pawnshop to steal musical instruments in hopes of organizing a band.

I was a young college music student from the University of Nebraska at Omaha and I rescued these young aspiring musicians from the court system.

I later instilled in these young men the importance of hard work, honesty and character development, as well as skills in musical performance; vital lessons that would later be used when they go into competition with more polished bands in the city. *A Bridge to Success* will touch your hearts and warm your soul as you see these young men and a generation of others progress from being at-risk to being productive members of our society.

Chuck Miller

1

THEIR MUSICAL COACH,

Photo courtesy of Chuck Miller

As a musical coach, musician, educator, author, conductor and music arranger, I Charles Lott Miller (a.k.a., Chuck Miller, Master Chazz) was born on January 17 in Prescott, Arkansas. I grew up in the Rice Quarters section of this town, which was named and owned by a white lady we called Miss Rice. I never did meet her but her name was always mentioned around the house. She owned most of the houses in this section except our house and a few others.

Photo courtesy of Chuck Miller

MY HOME & FAMILY EXPERIENCE

The Miller family lived in a little shotgun house located on West Vine Street. Our grandfather, Papa Lott Futch, lived across the street. Many family members and a few friends would gather at his house to play dominoes and card games almost every night. I remember when I was two or three years old, Mr. Rhody would carry me on his shoulder across the street to watch them play their games. I had lots of fun watching them play and most of all I enjoyed watching them share an evening of fun together. My late mother, Essie often said, "Papa let us play the games in order to keep his five girls close to home and away from bad boys in the neighborhood."

The neighborhood I grew up in was great. I played games with most of the kids who lived there, however; there were two boys who were not very friendly. Their names were Tootle-lu and John L. In fact, every time my sisters Wanda, Percy Mae and my late brother Freddy and I would go to the store to buy food for our mother, the two boys would make us give our store bought food to them. These boys were the neighborhood bullies, who in addition to taking our food took Wanda's bicycle. Boy, were we glad when they finally moved out of town.

I showed musical promise by age nine, singing for funerals and other church functions. My mother, a musician in her own rights, often accompanied me on piano. We always had an old piano in the house. Mother made sure that each of her five children learned how to play something on the piano. It was an old upright piano that sat in the front room. There were always some of the keys missing, but we played it anyway. Mother could really play. She was Munn Chapel Baptist Church's pianist for over thirty years.

All of the Miller children were very smart in school, especially the girls. Wanda was the Salutatorian of her class, and graduated from Nettleton Business College. She later married Willie Leroy Richardson, worked for Western Union and was honored for twenty-nine years of work at the Federal Reserve Bank of Kansas City in Omaha, Nebraska. She is pictured with her husband and family below:

Photo courtesy of Wanda Richardson

The Richardson Family.

Row 1, left to right: Myahni, Michael 3rd, Willie Richardson, Wanda Richardson, Kyrii, row 2, left to right: Ahmani, Monica, Lisa, Jaylyn, Camille, Lanaya, row 3 left to right: Shay, DeLAron, Michael Jr., Michael Sr., Kris, and Keelan.

3

My sister Percy tied with Kay Alice Walker as Valedictorian of her class. She later married Jesse Ray Hawthorne who is the Nephew of the legendary internationally known Blues singer, the late Jimmy Witherspoon. Her family is pictured below followed by Jimmy Witherspoon's photo and biography:

Photo courtesy of Percy Hawthorne

The Hawthorne Family.

Row 1, left to right: Jacquelyn, Jesse Ray Sr. and Percy Miller Hawthorne.
Row 2, left to right: The late Phillip Marcus and Jesse Ray Jr.

⅃⅃

Jimmy Witherspoon (Blues Singer 1923 - 1997):

James Witherspoon was born in _Gurdon, Arkansas_.[1] He first attracted attention singing with _Teddy Weatherford's_ band in _Calcutta, India_, which made regular _radio_ broadcasts over the U. S. _Armed Forces Radio Service_ during _World War II_. Witherspoon made his first _records_ with _Jay McShann's_ band in 1945. In 1949, recording under his own name with the McShann band, he had his first hit, _"Ain't Nobody's Business,_'[1] a song which came to be regarded as his signature tune. In 1950 he had hits with two more songs closely identified with him: "No Rollin' Blues", "Big Fine Girl", as well as "Failing By Degrees" and "New Orleans Woman" recorded with the Gene Gilbeaux Orchestra which included Herman Washington and Don Hill on the Modern Records label. These were recorded from a live performance on May 10, 1949 at a "Just Jazz" concert Pasadena, CA sponsored by Gene Norman. Another classic Witherspoon composition is "Times Gettin' Tougher Than Tough".

Witherspoon's style of blues - that of the _"blues shouter"_ - became unfashionable in the mid-1950s, but he returned to popularity with his 1959 album, Jimmy Witherspoon at the Monterey Jazz Festival, which featured _Roy Eldridge, Woody Herman, Ben Webster, Coleman Hawkins, Earl Hines_ and _Mel Lewis_, among others.[2] He later recorded with _Gerry Mulligan, Leroy Vinnegar, Richard "Groove" Holmes_ and _T-Bone Walker_.[1]

In 1961 he toured Europe with _Buck Clayton_ and returned to the UK on many occasions, featuring on a mid-sixties live UK recording Spoon Sings and Swings (1966) with tenor sax player _Dick Morrissey's_ quartet. In 1970, he appeared on _Brother Jack McDuff's_ London _Blue Note_ recording To Seek a New Home together with British jazz musicians, including _Terry Smith_ and _Dick Morrissey_. In the 1970s he also recorded the album _Guilty!_ (later released on CD as Black & White Blues) with _Eric Burdon_[1] and featuring Ike White & the San Quentin Prison Band. He then toured with a band of his own featuring _Robben Ford_ and _Russ Ferrante_. A _recording_ from this period, Spoonful, featured 'Spoon' accompanied by _Robben Ford_, _Joe Sample_, _Cornell Dupree_, _Thad Jones_ and _Bernard Purdie_.[3] He continued performing and recording into the 1990s.[3]

Other performers with whom Witherspoon recorded include _Jimmy Rowles_, _Earl "Fatha" Hines_, _Vernon Alley_, _Mel Lewis_, _Teddy Edwards_, _Gerald Wiggins_, _John Clayton_, _Paul Humphrey_, _Pepper Adams_, _Kenny Burrell_, _Harry "Sweets" Edison_, _Jimmy Smith_, _Long John Baldry_, _Junior Mance_, _Ellington bassist Jimmy Woode_, _Kenny Clarke_, _Gerry Mulligan_, _Jim Mullen_, _Count Basie_, Gene Gilbeaux and others.

Witherspoon died of _throat cancer_ in _Los Angeles, California_ on September 18, 1997.

http://en.wikipedia.org/wiki/Jimmy_Witherspoon (11 July 2010)[iii]

Photo courtesy of Percy M. Miller Hawthorne

Percy is an avail sports star. She played a great game of basketball in high school and later became an excellent bowler and in April 19, 1989, she was inducted into the Huntsville AWBA (Alabama Women's Bowling Association.), Hall of Fame, and later in July 5, 2009 she was inducted into the McRae High School Sports Hall of Fame in Prescott, Arkansas and was the first female to receive this honor.

All of my sisters and my brother were musically talented. The girls were great singers especially my younger sister Marchetta Louise Miller Fontaine. She not only has a great voice, her skills at playing the piano and synthesizer are amazing. Like her sister Percy, she married a relative of a professional singer; the late Davis Eli "David" Ruffin of the famous vocal group, the Temptations from the Motown Recording Corporation. David and her husband Tim Fontaine were very close. See the Fontaine's photo and Ruffin's photo and biography below:

Photo courtesy of Marchetta L. Miller Fontaine

The Fontaine Family.

Left to right: Tim, Matthew and Marchetta L. Miller Fontaine.

Davis Eli "David" Ruffin (January 18, 1941 – June 1, 1991) was an American soul singer and musician most famous for his work as one of the lead singers of the Temptations from 1964 to 1968 (or the group's "Classic Five" period as it was later known). He was the lead voice on such famous songs as "My Girl" and "Ain't Too

Proud to Beg." Known for his unique raspy and anguished tenor vocals, Ruffin was ranked as one of the 100 Greatest Singers of All Time by *Rolling Stone* magazine in 2008.

[1] He was inducted into the *Rock and Roll Hall of Fame* in 1989 for his work with the Temptations.[2] Fellow *Motown* recording artist *Marvin Gaye* once said admiringly of Ruffin that, "I heard in [his voice] a strength my own voice lacked." *http://en.wikipedia.org/wiki/David_Ruffin* (11 July 2010) [iv]

The Miller boys were great singers and instrumentalists. Freddy played the trombone and I played the trumpet. Here is a true story of how I began playing the trumpet. "Growing up in a single parent household, (my dad Percy and my mom Essie were separated), I was unable to study music privately and receive the musical attention many people now take for granted. Yet, I did manage to try out various instruments brought home by my brother Freddy. First I tried the flute, but I didn't like it; next I tried a clarinet, which did not suit me at all. The percussion was next, but this was not the one, and finally I tried the trumpet, and like the three bears, this was just right for me.

After playing the trumpet for only a few minutes, I was able to play the school's fight song, *"Our Boys Goanna Shine Tonight"* by ear. My performance on this piece was so structurally correct until Freddy suggested that I audition for the school's band director, Mr. Eddie Mullins. After passing the audition with flying colors, and although I was only the sixth grade, I was asked to join the McRae High School Marching Tigers Band.

Faced with the inability to purchase an instrument, I was forced to use one of the school's old hand me down trumpets. Armed with an early desire to succeed, I used that trumpet to play many of the first trumpet parts that heralded first place status in many of the school's music festivals.

The competition was very high at the festivals. Most of the musicians in the first trumpet section had shiny new trumpets with both silver and gold finishes. It was hard for me to sit in the section with my old outdated trumpet. My spirit to do my best was crushed. Nevertheless I managed to use this approach a few times; but then a miracle happened when my cousin Willie Arthur Smith loaned me his new trumpet. Using Willie's shiny new trumpet gave me a new sense of pride. I began playing the trumpet with a new desire to be the best in my school.

To be the best would cost me many long days and nights of practicing the trumpet. I would practice at school during free time; I would practice after school at band practice and I would practice as soon as I got home from band practice. I was always practicing. Sometimes I would spend entire Saturdays practicing. Sunday was reserved for worship so there was no practicing but I was always well prepared for the next band rehearsal.

It seemed as though every student had a special talent in our band. We had one of the best high school marching bands in the region. The McRae High School Marching Tigers won first place in many of the marching band contests held during the school year.

EARLY BANDS EXPERIENCE

Photo courtesy of Chuck Miller

The McRae High School Marching Tigers in 1957

Their Director, Eddie Mullins, standing, number one-front row right, me at age 12 (7th grade) standing behind Mr. Mullins, number one-second row right, and my brother Freddy age 14, standing, number four-second row left.

THE MOONLIGHTERS BAND

Performing has always played an important part in my life. My next move was to find a way to join the school's jazz combo (The Moonlighters). Although I was only in the sixth grade, there were two trumpet players in the seventh grade that were more experienced than I was.

However, with a great desire and determination, my new personal sound and true talent overshadowed the playing of the trumpeters and they relinquished their positions in the combo. Those guys are my heroes in playing the trumpet. I heard them play on many occasions. They inspire me even to this day.

Our pianist/band leader, the late Eddie Mullins formed the most successful instrumental/vocal group of young high school students in Prescott, Arkansas' history at McRae High School in 1957. He called his group The Moonlighters. This group performed for many of the proms, spring dances and other events held at McRae High and other schools within a fifty miles radius. To my knowledge, The Moonlighters was the first and only combo of it genre to formulate at McRae High.

Members of the original group were: The late Freddy L. Miller '60, trombone/vocals; Robert L. Anthony '60, piano, baritone horn, guitar and bass guitar; John A. Colbert '60, and the late Willie Charles Stuart '60, drums; James T. Mitchell and James Henry Marks '61, trumpets; and the late Royce Don Gilmore '61, tenor saxophone.

The group's classic line-up was established in 1958, when I, '62 replaced J.T. and James Henry. People say that I had a smooth tenor singing voice and my lyrical trumpet sound provided the perfect counterpoint to Royce's tenor saxophone sound and Freddy's trombone sound, a contrast that jazz trumpeter Miles Davis exploited to the fullest.

There were other members who joined later and carried on the torch, they were: Clemmie Joe Vanhook '63, guitar; Bertrum Garmon '63, trumpet, Cledis Stuart '64, tenor saxophone; Bobby Leroy Shaw '64, drums; the late Bernard Perry, guitar; Eddie Mullins Jr., trumpet, and the late Perry Anthony Jr.,

11

drums/vocals. Some class dates are unknown to this writer and there may have been others that were missed.

The Moonlighters provided entertainment for many of the young people in Prescott. The group performed many nights at The Hall, a skating rink owned by Mr. And Mrs. Ned Scott. Sometimes this was the only place in town where one could go and hear a live band play. They also performed many times in Nashville, Hope, Arkadelphia, Little Rock, Blevins, Gurdon, and many other small towns in Arkansas. This group stayed busy most weekends. Their manager made sure they represented the school favorably when they performed either in or out of town.

One milestone and a historical highlight for the Moonlighters were when we performed at the Armory and provided the entertainment for the first integrated social event in Prescott, Arkansas. We also performed for the first McRae High School Dinner Banquet held at the new campus.

As result of our performing experiences, the teaching and training received from McRae High, many of these students have since become professors, teachers, superintendents of public schools, church organists/vocalists, professional musicians/entertainers, news paper clerks and Pastors are a few of their occupations. The Moonlighters was one of the best instrumental combos during its time. The group is pictured below:

Photo courtesy of Chuck Miller

The Moonlighters, McRae High School, Prescott, Arkansas, 1957.

<u>Back row, from left to right</u>: Freddy L. Miller age 15, Robert L. Anthony age 15, James H. Marks age 14, me at age 13, and the late Royce D. Gilmore age 14, Front row, from left to right: John A. Colbert age 15 and Willie C. Stuart age 16.

MY FASCINATION WITH MARCHING BANDS

I was fascinated with bands of all types; I never missed an opportunity to watch a band perform. Although I attended a segregated school, it was an amazing experience to see local white marching bands perform in parades. Living only sixteen miles from where former President Bill Clinton was born and lived for a while, I often saw the Hope, Arkansas black Yeager High Marching Band as well as the Hope, Arkansas white High School Marching Band perform. Below is another photo of The Marching Tigers from the 1960's. Anita Pointer is shown playing the alto saxophone.

Photo courtesy of Chuck Miller

The McRae High School Marching Tigers in 1960.

Our Director, Eddie Mullins, standing, number one-row two right,
Chuck Miller at age 16, standing between baritone and tuba, center, row
three, my brother Freddy, standing, last row second from left playing tuba
and World famous Anita Pointer from the internationally
known group, The Pointer Sisters is standing row
three, second from left; playing the saxophone.

I performed in The Marching Tigers and The Moonlighters and gained a vast amount of experience, which led me to get the nerve to ask my mother and grandmother to buy me a trumpet of my own. This proved to be impossible, and as a result, James Tucker, a friend of my sister Wanda, bought me a used cornet from the Insurance man. James paid fifty dollars for the cornet, which didn't have a case.

You should have seen my face as I looked in the trunk of the Insurance man's car. I was the happiest boy around. This was not a new, shiny, long, well-kept trumpet, however, to me, this small, stubby, unpolished cornet without a case, was something special. It was the first brass musical instrument I ever owned. I played this instrument throughout high school and I even carried it to Hawaii when I joined the Army. This instrument is shown in the photo below:

Photo courtesy of Chuck Miller

The Fabulous Blazers, a group from Honolulu, Hawaii, 1963.

Left to right, row one: Unidentified bass player; Chuck Miller at age 19, holding his first owned cornet; unidentified guitar player. Left to right, row two: Unidentified drummer; Robin West, organ.

LEARNING TO PLAY THE PIANO

While stationed in Honolulu, Hawaii and assigned to work at Tripler General Army Hospital as a Medical Records Clerk and later as a Physical Examination Assistant, I became very serious about learning to play the piano. Each day, a soldier use to practice the piano at the Enlisted Men Service Club and he could play really well. I use to watch him practice through the window but I didn't have enough courage to approach him and ask for help.

Well, one day I got enough nerve to ask him to show me how to play some of the things he was practicing and to my surprise, he was happy to help me. The things he taught me are still with me today. He taught me the importance of both, learning how to read music and to play by ear (without music). I soon purchased me a little black spinet piano and begin practicing in a manner closely related to his routine.

Photo courtesy of Chuck Miller

Chuck Miller at age 21, sitting at my black spinet piano, 1965.

My family and I were one of the first families to move into the newly constructed Kuhio Park Terrace Apartments in Honolulu, Hawaii. I rented this piano from a local music store.

I would practice every day and each day I practiced, I got better and better. I remember being able to play standard tunes like: *"Dear Heart"*, *"Secret Love"*, *"My Bonnie Lie Over The Ocean"*, *"Good Night Ladies"* and a few others. This was a very exciting time in my life. In learning to play the piano, my life went to a new level and took on a new direction. My interest grew towards composing and arranging music. I think the reason I had such great success with the piano is because of the support from my wife, Chestene and our daughters, Connie, Cheryl and later Colette. They are pictured below:

Photos courtesy of Chestene Roberson Miller

Chestene Roberson Miller and daughters

Left to right: Chestene; Cheryl, Colette and Connie.

FAMILY SUPPORT IN OMAHA, NEBRASKA

Photo courtesy of Chestene Roberson Miller

The Miller Family.

<u>**Left to right**</u>: <u>**Row one**</u>: Chestene. Row two, left to right: JimNeshia Summer, Chuck, and NaTina. Row three, left to right & below: Branden, Johnathon, Eddie, Janique, and Essance.

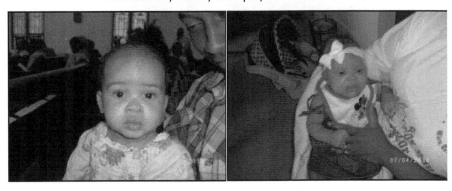

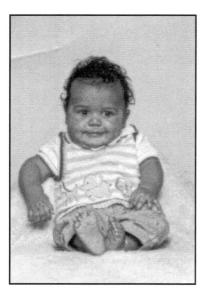

Photos courtesy of Chestene Roberson Miller & NaTina R. Miller.

The Connie Miller/Tucker Family.

Left to right: **Row one top**: Tykeshi. Row two, left to right: Robert Tucker 3rd, and Connie. Row three, left to right: Robert Tucker 4th, Dwight, Elias & De'Zha.

Photo courtesy of Cheryl L. Miller

The Cook Family.

Row one, front: Dominique Cook, Kevin Cook, and Diamond Cook.

Photo curtsey of Chestene Roberson Miller

The Miller, Carr, and Cook Families.

Row one, left to right: Dominique Cook, Amani Carr, NaTina Miller, and Diamond Cook. Row two, left to right: Branden Miller, JimNeshia Summer Miller and Donna Miller.

Photo courtesy of Chestene Roberson Miller

Number one from the front: Amani, NaTina and Jay.

Chuck Miller

Ariah

The Miller Family.

Row one left to right: Tykeshi, Cheryl, Diamond and JimNeshia Summer.
Row two left to right: NaTina, Johnathan, Donna, Chestene and Branden.
Row three: Eddie, Robert, Dwight and Chuck.

MY EMBARRASSING EXPERIENCE AT LETOES

After spending a three-year stint in the Armed Forces, I moved back to Omaha, Nebraska in 1966 and began working odd jobs, finished drafting school and finally landed a job working as a draftsman in Mod B at Offutt Air Force Base. My job duties centered on drawing cartoons for Mod B's Bulletin Boards.

This job proved to be enriching and important, however, my heart was still beating with the desire to succeed in some form of music. I would practice the piano during my lunch hour and during any break time.

During this time period, I was very much into the R&B music of James Brown, Bobby Blue Bland, and The Beatles. I knew all of the instrumental and vocal parts to their songs and felt very confident when ever I performed them. One night however, I met my match.

One night I went to this nightclub called Letoes (later called Mr. Green's, and much later, Back Street Lounge) to hear some live music. I took my trumpet in the club with me hoping to get a chance to play with the group. When I got there, the group was on break. I was lucky to get a seat right in front of the band and everyone could see that I had my trumpet with me. By the way, I was still carrying it in a paper bag; I still didn't have a case for it.

When the band members; who by the way were: (Billy Rogers on guitar, Donnie Beck on bass, and his twin brother Ronnie Beck on drums) returned from their break, someone introduced me by saying, there is a new trumpet player in town and he wants to set in with the group tonight.

Chuck Miller

Photos courtesy of Chuck Miller

Photo courtesy of Chuck Miller

Three of the most talented musicians in Omaha, 1966.

These photos were taken many years later. Pictured from left to right: Billy Rogers, Donnie Beck and Ronnie Beck.

Everyone clapped and shouted yea, for me and I went to the stage. Little did I know that the band that was playing that night was a jazz band. I had never heard of this kind of a band before as I thought everyone played the music of James Brown or Bobby Blue Bland and others.

Anyway, they kicked the song off and they played through the head or melody of the song and then it was my time to play a jazz solo. It was so embarrassing; I didn't know what to play! I didn't know the name of the song or anything, I was stuck! After they played their solos, played the head and ended the song, I took my seat. I had never felt so low in my life. People looked at me with a since of pity. I don't remember anyone laughing out loud at me but I am sure they did it silently.

The good thing about this is, it taught me a lesson. I must learn this new style of music. I tried asking the group to tell me the name of the song and where could I find the recording, but they told me, they had made the song up. I really didn't believe them and later found out that the name of the song was *Milestones* by Miles Davis.

SOLO TRANSCRIPTION ASSIGNMENT

A few months later, a drummer by the name of Freddy Waits from Florida came to Omaha while on tour and stayed a while. We became good friends and he gave me my first jazz assignment, to learn the solo of Miles Davis' song, guess what song it was? Yes, *Milestones*.

Freddy had no idea what had taken place a few months earlier at Leatos, but managed to bring a revelation into my life through this particular assignment. I recognized the song right away and was a little angry with that group for quite sometime.

When Freddy gave me this assignment, I was real nervous. I was nervous because I really didn't know how to do what he asked me to do. I had never transcribed a jazz solo before and didn't think I could do it. Well I was right! But guess what happened? He gave me two weeks to do the assignment. After the time was up, I took my results to him and guess what he said? "This is great man! You did a great job!"

There were erasure marks all over the paper and none of the notes seem correct. However, Freddy complimented me on my effort. I had tried and had done my best, which would bring a great reward in the future. As a result of that assignment, I became if not the best, one of the best transcribers of music in the Omaha Metro area, thanks to Freddy.

NEW BANDS

I later heard the music of the late great tenor saxophonist John Coltrane for the first time. I was so excited to hear music of this genre until I kept trying to learn how to play it every day. My first best friend, guitarist, Jack Murrell introduced me to this group. Jack and I have remained best friends even until this day in 2010. See Jack and his family in the photo below:

Photo courtesy of Chuck Miller

Jack Murrell and his family in Omaha, 1966.

Pictured from left to right: Jack Murrell, (holding his son, Quinton), his wife, Choice and their daughter, Janie, their daughter Jackie and an unborn Jack Jr., not pictured.

Blake and the Manderson's Band

The first band I joined when I moved back to Omaha was a group called, Blake & The Mandersons; I am pictured below at the synthesizer. Notice my trumpet-mute standing on the synthesizer and my trumpet is lying on the amplifier on my right. The most popular songs we played were *"Mustang Sally"* and *"Wait till the Midnight Hour"* by Wilson Picket. The group is pictured below:

Photo courtesy of Chuck Miller
Blake & the Mandersons', Nov., 1967.

Left to right: Clarence O'Neal, bass, George, tenor saxophone, me at age 23, trumpet & electric piano, Jack Murrell, electric piano, not pictured, Herman Franklin, guitar, Al Walker, drums.

The New Breed of Soul Band

Photo courtesy of Chuck Miller
Andre Davis, Manager of
The Newbreed of Soul, Dec., 1967.

I later joined a group called the New Breed of Soul, managed by Andre Davis, a DJ from Detroit, Michigan. Andre is great friends with vocal groups, Martha and the Vandellas and The Four Tops. They all went to the same school in Detroit. He is pictures in the photo on the Left.

This group played in and out of town and was fortunate to perform at the famous nightclub in downtown Omaha called Mickey's. Our most popular songs were *"Knock on Wood"* by Sam & Dave" and *"Try a little Tenderness"* by Otis Redding. See the group pictured below.

Photo courtesy of Chuck Miller

The Newbreed of Soul, Dec., 1967.

Left to right: Clarence 3X, drums, Herman Franklin, lead guitar, Richard Chatman, rhythm guitar, Chuck Miller at age 23, trumpet, and Leroy Montgomery, bass.

The Persuaders Band

I next joined a group under the leadership of Eddie Gaines called The Persuaders. The group is pictured below. Soon I became the new leader of the Persuaders and the group later became one of the most popular groups in the city during this time.

Photo courtesy of Chuck Miller

The Original Persuaders, 1968.

Left to right: Eddie Gaines, drums, Steven Smith, trumpet, Dale Smith, bass, Robert Whitemon, tenor saxophone, Me at age 24, trumpet and flute, Lois McMoris, guitar, and Earl Page, organ, (not pictured).

Photo courtesy of Chuck Miller

The Persuaders at Gino's Night Club, 1968.

Note unidentified Go Go Dancers. Musicians left to right: Earl Page, organ, Johnny Butler, vocals, me at age 24, trumpet, Billy Love, drums, Sam Singleton, vocals, Keith Nelson, guitar, Eric Johnson, bass, and Chris Lombardo, saxophone, (not pictured).

Keith Nelson, the group's guitarist was a student at Omaha University (OU). He was one of the major forces, which influenced me to go to college. It happened while we were on the road one day. We were all riding in the van to a gig when Keith told me I should register for college and major in music. At first I didn't think it was possible, but as I thought about it, I said why not? I finally made the decision to try and attend Omaha University in the summer of 1969.

2

NEW EXPERIENCES AT OU & NEW MUSICIANS, 1969-73

MY FIRST ADVICE ABOUT PREJUDICE AND OTHER EXPERIENCES

Photo courtesy of Chuck Miller
Elmer Charles "Basie" Givens. My first Counselor before attending UNO.

By the summer of 1969 the word had spread throughout the city that I had made plans to enroll in Omaha University's Music Department Program. It was Elmer Charles "Basie" Givens (one of Omaha's most gifted bass players at the time) who enlightened me that some people in the Music Department were prejudice and that many of our most gifted local African American musicians had tried to graduate from the Department with limited success.

Basie went on to advise me to enroll with the thought of graduating and not letting the acts of prejudice force me to quit the way it had forced others before me. I was convinced that this was not going to stop me. Mr. Givens' words have remains with me until this day. Armed with his advice, and a written recommendation letter from the late Paul Allen of Allen Showcase; I passed a trumpet audition for my mentor and band director, Mr. Reginald Schive. I was gladly accepted and welcomed into Omaha University (OU) later to be called, The University of Nebraska at Omaha (UNO's) instrumental music program. This was a great opportunity for me to expand my writing and arranging skills as well as my trumpet and keyboard skills.

After attending a few classes and trying to feed my desire to learn how to play jazz, there was only one incidence which showed a degree of prejudice and that was with Dr. Peterson.

Photo courtesy of Chuck Miller

Dr. James Peterson, UNO Music Department Chairman, 1969.

Photo courtesy of Chuck Miller

It all happened this way. One day a former University classmate, Percy Marion (see photo above) and I were sitting in a classroom trying to learn how to play jazz chords on the piano, when we were told, by the Music Department Head, Dr. Peterson, *"We don't play that kind of music out here"*.

Being freshmen at the time, we became frighten, stop playing the piano and left the room. I later went home and told my wife Chestene what Dr. Peterson said and she asked me, "Are you going to school to please that man or are you going there to get an education?"

I thought about what she said and I returned alone to the classroom the next day and started to practice jazz again.

When Dr. Peterson stuck his head in the classroom door I immediately asked him, with a stern voice, what do you want? Dr. Peterson literally ran out of the doorway and he never confronted me again. After that incident, we begin freely to practice jazz on campus any time we wanted too, this was indeed a turning point in the Music Department's policy or thoughts on what kind of music could be played on the UNO campus.

NEW MUSICIANS AND NEW BANDS

When things cooled down a little, I formed a jazz group called The Chuck Miller Sextet, named after the Miles Davis Sextet. I formed the group with Marcus McLaurine on bass, (now plays bass for the legendary trumpeter Clark Terry), Payton Crossley on drums, (played drums with legendary pianist Amad Jamal and now with legendary bassist Ron Carter), Archie Parks on organ and piano, Rich Cornell on alto saxophone, the late Percy Marion on tenor saxophone, (moved on to attend Berklee College of Music in Boston, Mass., and later joined The Legendary Duke Ellington Orchestra) and I played the trumpet.

Photo courtesy of Chuck Miller

Marcus McLaurine, bass.

Photo courtesy of Chuck Miller

Payton Crossley, drums.

We were a carbon copy of the Miles Davis Sextet who had "Philly" Joe Jones on drums, Red Garland on piano, Paul Chambers on bass, Julian "Cannonball" Adderly on alto saxophone, John Coltrane on tenor saxophone and Miles Davis on trumpet.

The sextet group performed various noontime concerts at UNO, which were free and opened to the student body. This happened way before the Student Program Organization (SPO) opened it's programming to jazz groups on campus. Whether my jazz group lead directly or indirectly to jazz being played on UNO's campus, it did predate any such actions. My group performed jazz on the campus in 1969; Rick David explained SPO's new activities plans in the winter of 1970-71. Here is a quoted passage from the 1970-71 Tomahawk Year book.

⌐

Stop, look, listen (SPO Re-Groups):

"Off to a slow start this year, the Student Programming Organization (SPO) will put its revamped activity program to test second semester. A spring concert featuring Sly and the Family Stones or Santana, a jazz festival headlined by Cannonball Adderly or Jimmy Smith, a black symposium generated through Black Studies Coordinator Melvin Wade and at least one lecture by a controversial national figure such as Ralph Nader, Billy Russell or Erich Fromm is on the planning table.

Offsetting the jolt felt by SPO after the Ides of March Homecoming concert cancellation are new ideas, better organization and planning. Much of SPO's new image centers on Student Activities Coordinator Rick David. David, who took over part of the responsibilities of former Student Activities Director Fred Ray, is attempting to shape SPO into an organization that will work for all UNO students rather than the interest of only a few factions." <u>UNO Tomahawk p. 55.</u> [vi]

⌐

CHUCK MILLER & THE PERSUADERS BAND

While attending UNO, I continued performing pretty much the way Miles Davis performed. Sometimes he would play jazz and then he would play fusion/rock. I played jazz with the Sextet and then switched to funk/soul. I started performing with the Persuaders group again, however; this time, the group's name was changed to Chuck Miller & the Persuaders do to contracts reasons. It was popular during this time to have someone with credibility lead the group.

Dancing With A "Soul Band"

CHUCK MILLER & THE PERSUADERS

Members of Chuck Miller & The Persuaders: From left to right (front row) are John Butler, Chuck Miller, Sam Singleton, and Eric Johnson. From left to right (back row) are Earl Page, Keith Nelson and Eddie Gaines.

"Dancing In The Dark"   "Unforgettable"

Fairbury Junior College lads and lasses had an enjoyable evening this month while dancing by the delicate "SOUL MUSIC" of CHUCK MILLER & THE PERSUADERS. The event was the annual Homecoming Ball at which the Miller ensemble was invited to perform.

Photo courtesy of Chuck Miller

Chuck Miller age 25 & the Persuaders, 1969.

Note, the group's name has been changed to Chuck Miller & The Persuaders and Eddie Gaines number three left to right back row, replaces Billy Love on Drums.

THE UNIVERSITY OF NEBRASKA MARCHING BAND

At UNO in 1970, I performed in many of the orchestras, stage bands (jazz ensembles) and marching bands.

Photo courtesy of UNO Year Book[vii]

The University of Nebraska Marching Band, 1970.

Note row one number one left to right, guitarist Keith Nelson from Chuck Miller & the Persuaders group. Row three, me at age 26, second from right; Row six, The late Percy Marion, second from left.

The 1970's were a busy time for me, performing in many local groups including The Persuaders. Leroy Enhofe replaced Keith Nelson on guitar and the group's name was reduced from Chuck Miller and the Persuaders back to the Persuaders. Sam Singleton, the group's lead singer had a problem with me being featured. He said that he was the entertainer in the group and I was the musician.

He wanted his name to replace mine but the group would not go for that being that I was the leader and the one who arranged all of the music and the engagements. I soon agreed with him and asked that my name be removed and that was that. Following is a photo of the Persuaders with Leroy present.

Photo courtesy of Chuck Miller

The Persuaders, 1970.

Note the group's name has been changed back to the Persuaders and drummer Billy Love returned to the group. Billy is sitting number four left to right row one. Other members are, left to right, row one: Earl Page organ, Leroy Enhofe guitar, me at age 26 trumpet, left to right, row two: Johnny Butler lead vocals, Eric Johnson bass, and Sam Singleton lead vocals.

In 1971 Marcus, Payton and I formed The Chuck Miller Quartet by adding Tom Hennig on electric piano. This group performed mostly at The Black Hawk Lounge on 24th Street. Gerald Holts later replaced Marcus on bass, this proved to be a most rewarding move.

Being that we were all very young musicians, trying to learn how to play jazz, the presence of jazz veterans Holts and Hennig made our music sound more professional which helped increase clientele at the club.

POVERTY'S MOVEMENT BAND

Members from the group The Persuaders formed a new group called Poverty's Movement. The group recorded a new 45 R. PM entitled, "Heartbreak."

This group came a long way in a short time, and they continued to grow as time passed. The group was composed

of five males and one female. At the time, they were considered to be the best all around band in the Midwest.

Not only could they make you pat your feet to the sound of soul but also they were one of a few groups that inserted choreography into their routine. The group is shown in the photo below:

Photo courtesy of Chuck Miller

Poverty's Movement, 1972.

Left to right, row one: Roosevelt Collins, organ;
Chuck Miller age 28, trumpet & vocals; Garie Crowder, bass; Hank Thomas, tenor saxophone & vocals; Larry Smith, drums; Lois Eleby, guitar & vocals; and Johnny Butler, vocals.

THE LUIGI WAITES JAZZ QUINTET

As we developed in the performance of jazz, I later in 1972 joined the Luigi Waites Jazz Quintet. Members in this group were: Luigi on drums, Marcus McLaurine on bass, Tom Hennig on piano, Dave Paulson on tenor saxophone and I played trumpet. I was now moving up in the jazz world.

All of these musicians were very well known and very talented. This group was the first group to play at The Howard Street Tavern, one of the few jazz clubs located downtown in The Old Market. Luigi is shown in the photo below:

http://en.wikipedia.org/wiki/Luigi_Waites[viii]

The Late Luigi Waites.

This is where members of the group talents really grew. It grew because there was a jam session each weekend during our gig at Howard Street. One time jazz veteran trumpeter and saxophonist Red Higgins came and set in with us. We were playing a Blues in F by organist Jimmy Smith and Red gave me the best compliment ever, he told me to keep doing what I was doing because I sounded like jazz trumpeter Clifford Brown when I played my solo.

This was a great compliment because it came from one of the greatest musicians in the Omaha area. Red later played the trumpet and helped me record one of my original songs. Red had the most beautiful sound when he played the trumpet, so lyrical and melodic. He also played the tenor saxophone and he is the reason I begin playing the tenor saxophone in my groups.

Red moved from Chicago to Omaha with Legendary tenor saxophonist Red Holloway back in the 1950's. I really miss him; he really blessed my heart when he made the recording for me. See Red Higgins in the photo below:

Photo courtesy of Chuck Miller

Red Higgins.

Bennie Harris replaced Marcus on bass, Sherman Johnson joined us on trombone and King Richard joined us on guitar. We played a few jobs at Slim Jenkins place, an after hours club, before we disbanded. Sherman later became manager for one of my groups and Bennie, King Richard and I later played in the Bennie Harris Quintet.

I played in Luigi's band during the weekends and played in UNO's Jazz Big Band during the week. I remember one concert we played for the Department of Music and Epsilon Omega Chapter of Phi Mu Alpha Sinfonia Sorority in November 29, 1972.

Many of my friends were in that band. Dave Polson played lead alto saxophone, Don Hatfield played tenor saxophone and flute, John Kirsch, Bob Brabec and I played trumpet, Eddie Russo and Tony Gulizia played trombone, Tony also played piano, Joey Gulizia and Rick Weiner played percussion. What a group that was. Our director was my mentor Reginald Schive, not only a director but also a friend to all of the musicians.

A few months later, while still attending UNO, I begin working part time at the Gene Eppley North Omaha Boys Club; my duties were centered on Arts and Crafts. I worked under the leadership of Bob Colby who was the Cultural Arts Director at the time; what a great boss he was. I really learned a lot from him and I later replaced him as Cultural Arts Director a few years later.

While working at the Boys' Club, I organized a new version of the group Poverty's Movement. This time Vernon Martin replaced Johnny Butler as lead vocalist. This was a very hot group. One of our favorite songs was a song recorded by Bobby Womack called "*Close to you.*" The thing that made our performance on this song different was; I wrote the string parts for the horns.

The horns played the string parts and the regular horn part as a part of our horn arrangement. This made us sound different from all of the other bands. They tried, but they were unsuccessful in figuring out how we got our beautiful horn arrangement. This group is shown in the photo below:

Photo courtesy of Chuck Miller

Poverty's Movement Band, 1973.

Left to right: Hank Thomas, tenor saxophone & vocals; Garie Crowder, bass; Larry Smith, drums; Roosevelt Collins, organ; Chuck Miller age 29, trumpet & vocals; Vernon Martin, vocals; and Lois Eleby, guitar & vocals.

3

MEETING MY MUSIC HEROES

Nineteen seventy three was a busy year for me and what a year that was. All the dreams I had in wanting to meet my music heroes were fulfilled. In January, I met jazz trumpeter Dizzy Gillespie, in February, I met trumpeter Eddie Henderson, pianist Herbie Hancock, in March, I was fortunate to meet jazz pianist Count Basie and jazz trumpeter Clark Terry at the same time, and in April, I met pianist Joe Zawinul, and Wayne Shorter. I next met jazz guitarist Kenny Burrell. Much later, I met jazz trumpeter Wynton Marsallis and I took photos with my friends Anita Pointer and her sisters from the famous Pointers Sister singing group. These individuals are shown in the photos below:

Photo courtesy of Chuck Miller

Jazz trumpeter, Dizzy Gillespie.

Photo courtesy of Chuck Miller

Chuck Miller and jazz trumpeter, Eddie Henderson.

Photo courtesy of Chuck Miller

Jazz pianist, Herbie Hancock and Chuck Miller.

Photo courtesy of Chuck Miller

Jazz pianist Joe Zawinul and Chuck Miller.

Photo courtesy of Chuck Miller

Count Basie, Chuck Miller and Clark Terry.

Photo courtesy of Chuck Miller

Chuck Miller, Count Basie, and Lou Moore.

Photo courtesy of Chuck Miller

Chuck Miller and jazz trumpeter, Clark Terry.

Photo courtesy of Chuck Miller

Jazz Saxophonist, Wayne Shorter, and Chuck Miller.

Photo courtesy of Chuck Miller

Chuck Miller and jazz trumpeter, Wynton Marsalis.

Photo courtesy of Chuck Miller

The Pointer Sisters.

Standing from left to right: June, Ruth, Chuck and Anita.

I had the pleasure of opening a concert at U.N.O. for jazz guitarist Kenny Burrell. For this performance I used a group called, *The Jazz All-stars*. These were some of the best musicians in town. There was Stemzy Hunter on alto saxophone, Jerry Davis on guitar, Gerald Holts on bass, Tom Hennig on piano, Jeff Ray on Congas, Payton Crossley on drums and I played trumpet.

What a group this was. We had it all. Everyone could play his part and on top of that, everyone could solo very well. I paid these musicians $100.00 for only one hour of performance. This was great money during this time. I was happy to be able to pay them an amount that would make them happy.

Kenny was very impressed with our performance. He even asked me how long I had left before graduating from U.N.O. I later met Kenny at U.C.L.A. in Los Angeles, California at a jazz workshop. We talked and reminisced about the performance at U.N.O. Below is a photo of The Jazz All-stars in concert at U.N.O.

Photo courtesy of Chuck Miller

The Jazz Altars; opening for Jazz Guitarist Kenny Burrell, 1973.

From left to right: Tom Hennig, piano; Jeff Ray, percussion; Gerald Holts, bass; Stemzy Hunter, alto saxophone; Payton Crossley, drums; Chuck Miller age 29, trumpet, and Jerry Davis, guitar.

Meeting Kenny Burrell was a great treat. He is so kind and gentle, a man who is concerned about the welfare of others. Kenny and I are pictured in the photo below.

Opening for Kenny and later world-renowned jazz organist, Jimmy Smith is something I will never forget. I regret that I don't have a picture with Jimmy; I remember, standing right there close to his Hammond B-3 organ with my trumpet in my hand. He and Kenney Burrell asked me the same question, "how long do I have left in school?"

Photo courtesy of Chuck Miller

Chuck Miller and Jazz guitarist, Kenny Burrell, 1973.

4

THE FABULOUS RHINESTONES TOUR THE U.S.

The Fabulous Rhinestones, 1973.

*Kal David, guitar, Harvey Brooks bass and
Marty Grebb, saxophone & keyboards.*

In October of 1973, I took a leave of absence from UNO and
the Boys Club and went to New York with Stemzy Hunter to join
an R&B-based band called *The Fabulous Rhinestones*. The
leader was Harvey Brooks, a bassist who had recorded with

Miles Davis on his Bitches Brew album; Brooks was well acquainted with the music industry. Other members of the group were guitarist Kal David, organist and saxophonist Marty Grebb, drummer Jack Scarangella and saxophonist Stemzy Hunter. Three members are shown in the photo above:

http://www.raremp3.co.uk/2010/06/fabulous-rhinestones-freewheelin-1973.html[ix] (12 July 2010).

The following Biography is from the Internet:

⌐

The Fabulous Rhinestones were an R&B-based band formed in San Francisco in 1971 by ex-Illinois Speed Press guitarist/singer Kal David and ex-Electric Flag (and Bob Dylan, Al Kooper, and Miles Davis) bassist Harvey Brooks. They moved to Woodstock, NY, where they played with members of the Band and some of their own fellow Chicago bluesmen, including Paul Butterfield, and were signed by producer Michael Lang -- the co-producer of the Woodstock festival -- to his own Just Sunshine label. The group cut three LPs over the next three years, all of which received critical raves without selling in huge numbers -- they also got considerable exposure playing on the same bill with the Allman Brothers, Stevie Wonder, and the Doobie Brothers, but their most visible gig was probably playing a 1971 antiwar rally in New York with John Lennon and Yoko Ono. They split up in the mid-'70s and David later played with Etta James, Al Kooper, and Johnny Rivers. The Fabulous Rhinestones' work has been compiled for reissue on CD in Japan in the 21st century. ~ Eder, Bruce, All Music Guide. http://www.cmt.com/artists/az/fabulous_rhinestones/bio.jhtml[x] (12 July 2010).

⌐

After rehearsing for about two weeks, the group went on tour to promote its new album. The Rhinestones left Newark, New Jersey on October 27 on National flight # 125 at 9:45 a.m. and arrived in Orlando, Florida at 12:00 noon. We stayed at the Ramada

Inn, Orlando Altamonte Springs. We played an out door concert at the Seminole Turf Club with Don Cooper and Loggins & Messina.

On October 28, we left Orlando and went to St. Petersburg and stayed at the Holiday Inn-South. The same line-up performed a concert at the Bayfront Center Auditorium. The following evening at 5:55 p.m. we boarded Eastern Ail Lines # 164 out of Tampa and arrived at JFK-New York City air terminal at 8:21 p.m.

On November 21, Stemzy and I left LaGuardia Air Terminal United flight # 215 at 6:00 p.m. and arrived in Omaha at 8:10 p.m. We stayed in Omaha six days before leaving for Las Angeles, California. We left Omaha Tuesday November 27 on United flight #535 at 11:10 a.m. and arrived in L.A. International Air Terminal at 12: 15 p.m.

We later checked into the Continental Hyatt House on Sunset Blvd. in Hollywood to get a good night's rest. The next evening on November 28-December 2, we performed to a sell out crowd at the Whisky A Go Go Night Club in Hollywood.

Everything was going great. The next day on December 3, we left L.A. International Air Terminal on Western Flight # 606 at 2:30 p.m. and arrived in San Francisco, California. We stayed at the Continental Vagabond Lodge on Van Ness Street. We performed at the Lion Share on December 7-8, at The Orphanage Club on December 9-11.

This is where Sylvester "Sly" Stone from the group Sly & The Family Stone came to watch us perform. Sly was there because Jack Scarengella use to be his drummer and he wanted to check the group out.

At 6:30 p.m., on Wednesday December 12, we left San Francisco on Western Air Lines flight # 96 and arrived in Denver, Colorado at 9:37 p.m. We stayed at the Holiday Inn downtown and performed at the Town & Country Lodge later that evening.

On Thursday December 13, we taped a Radio Broadcast for KFML Radio before performing our last performance with The Fabulous Rhinestones band at Ebbetts Field nightclub. On December 17, 1973 Stemzy and I returned to Omaha in time for Christmas and New Years Celebrations.

This ended our contract with the Rhinestones. What a great experience we received with this group. This was the best professional group I had ever performed with. I shall remember this experience forever.

MORE THAN A MUSIC TEACHER

To the Omaha community, I became more than a music teacher; I became a personal musical coach who continues to provide perspectives, ideas, options, and encouragement to all of my students. It has been said that my teachings has helped three generations of students from all over Omaha to become not only better musicians but better citizens as a whole.

Developing students became good students, good students became great students, and great students ventured out into the world becoming musicians, actors, businessmen and women, and lawyers sharing the stage with many of our professionals in the work arena.

A year later, when I returned to UNO, I performed with internationally known jazz saxophonists Grover Washington Jr. and, Arnie Lawrence. A writer from the Metro News Paper wrote the following comments about my performance with Lawrence:

⌐

"Lawrence played a jazz improvisation around the melody of Hucklebuck with Chuck Miller, who is working toward his Bachelors degree at UNO. Miller approached Lawrence after most of the others had left the lecture room. "When I was playing with you...the warmth man. I just felt it," Miller said. Lawrence said few musicians of Miller's ability had attended his clinics. "I was surprised when I heard those beautiful rich sounds," Lawrence said." The Metro News Paper, Week of March 14, 1974.[xi]

⌐

See the two as they perform in the photo below:

Photo courtesy of Metro News Paper

Miller and Lawrence.' I felt the warmth', 1974.

From left to right: Miller age 30, trumpet; Melvin Hall, bass guitar; Roger, guitar; Arthur Chernac, guitar, and Lawrence create beautiful melodies.

After the workshop was over, Arnie asked me to perform with him and the University Jazz Ensemble in the evening's concert. I accepted and what a good time I had. Here I was; not yet a member of the Jazz Ensemble, yet he asked me to join him in the concert, what a privilege that was.

Chuck Miller Quintet plus One Band

A nice article was written about my next group in the U.N.O. Gateway News Paper, see the article below:

Ⅼ

The headlines in The U.N.O. Gateway News Paper read: "Chuck Miller Quintet Likes to Communicate." I was quoted as saying: "the only purpose of our group is to make people happy." And Chuck Miller, of the Chuck Miller Quintet, will attempt to make the people at SPO coffeehouse happy on October 31 and November 1, 1974.

The quintet, formed only six months ago, has had a surprising amount of exposure. One week after the group materialized, they appeared on a telethon. One month after that, they went on Expressions with Bob Reynolds. Since then, the group has done a show for Nebraska Educational Television (ETV), which is called; Jazz Is Alive and Well, which, Chuck said, would appear sometimes in December.

When the group isn't appearing on television, they are performing at the Black-hawk Lounge, 24th and Laird, where, according to Miller, they have an indefinite contract. Although together only a short time, the band has had several personnel changes. The original quintet had six members, which was called the Chuck Miller Quintet plus One. See the group's photo below:

Photo courtesy of Chuck Miller

Chuck Miller Quintet plus One, NETV, 1974.

From left to right: King Richard, guitar; unidentified bass player; Eddie Russo, Trombone; Hank Davis, drums; Chuck Miller, trumpet; and John Jamison, synthesizer.

The group is now down to five, with the original bass player now attending the Boston Berkley School of Music, and the drummer now playing for Billy Rogers and Lonnie Smith, a well-known jazz organist. Tom Hennig came to the group as pianist. Miller doesn't think the desertion have hurt the group. "It was no loss because when I got them (the original musicians), they were just learning. It was a training period, and I'm glad it's over." Miller said the quintet started off as an experimental group to learn jazz. This experiment led to a regular job at the Black-hawk on Tuesday nights. U.N.O. Gateway News Paper, Week of October 25, 1974.[xii]

Leonard Harris later replaced John Jameson on organ, Eddie Russo trombone, Curley Martin percussionist and Chuck Miller trumpet/vocals.

Photo courtesy of Chuck Miller

The Chuck Miller Quintet plus One.

From left to right: Row one, Gerald Holts, bass; Curley Martin, drums; "King" Richard Gardner, guitar; Eddie Russo, trombone; Leonard Harris, organ; and Chuck Miller, trumpet.

After performing with The Chuck Miller Quintet Plus One and the change of personnel, I was ready to conquer the world. I was ready to take on a new assignment, which brought me back to The North Omaha Boys' Club.

5

LIFE AT THE BOYS CLUB

A RAY OF HOPE

After the tour of the US with The Fabulous Rhinestones; during this new year of January 1975, I reenrolled at The University of Nebraska at Omaha; and I also started working again at The North Omaha Boys Club. Everything seemed different. The cries among African American children and others across the country during the mid 1970's were a cry of despair.

Many were without fathers in the home, lived in drug infested environments, gang units in the Omaha, Nebraska area were just beginning to recruit its earliest victims and hope for many of our children was nowhere to be found. This was a disturbing picture. Something had to be done to help. I wanted to offer help by bringing change and hope into the lives of these hurting children.

Photo courtesy of Chuck Miller

Chuck Miller & Clarence Nichols, 1975.

Chuck age 31, ready to give a ray of hope to hurting children of Omaha.

My plan was to start a music program by designing an original curriculum that would teach kids the basics of music and help them develop positive self-discipline skills at the same time. A good friend of mine, the late James Drue Benson, who by the way was about the same age as my mother, told me about a job opening at The Gene Eppley North Omaha Boys Club. The position called for someone who could design and head a Music Department. I applied and accepted the job.

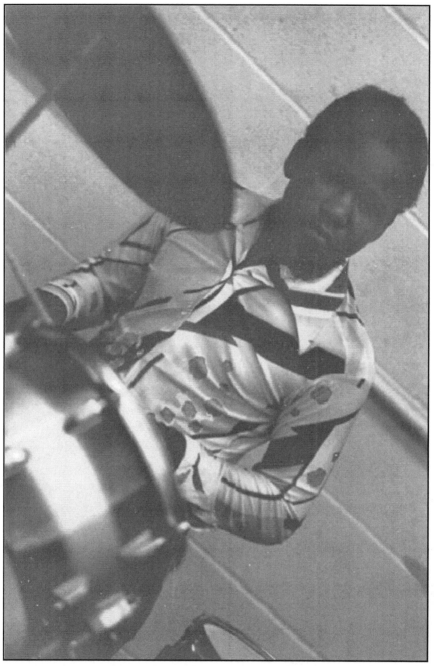

Photo courtesy of Chuck Miller
Boys Club's drummer. Mark "Bam-Bam" McKee.

Photo courtesy of Chuck Miller

Chuck Miller & James Drue Benson, 1975

Left to right: Chuck Miller & James Drue Benson.
Mrs. Helen Pinkard is in the rear.

Breaking into a Pawn Shop

They dreamed of one day performing in a band on stage. In the summer of **1975** a group of teenaged at-risk boys stood under a street light on Evans Street in Omaha, Nebraska and talked about putting a band together.

Having no instruments and no way of acquiring them, they wondered up and down the sidewalks of down town Omaha, looking at instruments in store windows, hoping someday they would get a chance to own an instrument. They began hanging around a boy named Kevin who taught them how to steal cars. With this new knowledge, they began planning how they could steal not only cars but musical instruments.

One night as they stood in their favorite spot on Evans Street, they did something they had never done before; they planned an event that would change their lives forever. They broke into a Pawn Shop and stole some musical instruments.

I began my mission by rescuing these young men from the court system after they robbed a pawnshop and stole musical instruments in order to start a band. Going to court with these young men was a new experience for me and for them. I remember sitting there in the court room listening to the judge explain to the boys about the consequences they could face for this crime. She told them never to come into her courtroom again unless they wanted to end up in jail for a long time.

IL

Eye Rock
April 2008
New York City

The late Calvin Howell (The Boys Club's first bass guitar student):

"One summer, a few of our future band buddies decided to take matters into their own hands. There was a music store near downtown, Sol's Music store I think was the name. They were a pawnshop as well as a music store and had all kinds of great equipment, all stacked up for the taking.

They broke right through the front Glass door. I think they used a sledgehammer or axe to break the glass. Of course, there was an alarm but their plan was to get in, grab, and get out with some nice guitars and amps and other band equipment.

The heist actually was a success. However, the next day, I got a call to come over to a friend house where most of the goods were kept. He wanted to give me one of the amps. Man, I was so nervous; all I had to do was to take the amp to my house right across the street!

I put the amp in my basement and I enjoyed playing through it for two or three days. By the second or third day, as I looked out of the window of our house, I saw a Police car pull up to my friend's house. In addition to the Police car, there were a couple of under cover Police cars there also.

As they got out of their cars, and walked up to the front door, they went into his house! Oh no! I panicked! I ran downstairs to our basement, got out that amp, and hustled it out the back door and put the amp by the back fence behind our garage.

Then I thought what if the cops came over to look around for that extra amp at my house? So, I jumped the fence with the amp and hid it in the weeds behind the row of houses that faced 24th street. Then, I went back into my room and watched out the window in horror as I saw the Police coming out of my friend's house with the very equipment we planned to make our careers with.

They took my friend downtown and I thought I was going to die as I thought the guys would squeal and tell them I had one of the amps. Well, the Police never came to my house. They let him go as they had recovered substantially all of the stolen goods.

I wondered how did the Police know where to look for the equipment? How in the world did they know it was our group of friends, all of us juveniles without any criminal records, had pulled off this heist? Well, in the next few days, it would all come to light.

One of our so-called friends had gotten greedy and gone out again with some other guys to try and score some more equipment from a music store up on Dodge Street. Well, those guys got busted the same night! When they took them downtown, the detectives asked if they knew anything about the Sol's Music break-in. So, it was our close friend who ratted out my neighbor and our crew and sent the cops directly to Evans Street and to his house where the equipment was being held.

Chuck Miller, the new Boys' Club Music teacher had to go to court with the fellows and as the results of a kind hearted female Judge the boys were ordered to join the music program in place of receiving jail time. This was their lucky break, to receive only a stern warnings and a chance to succeed as musicians.

When things settled down, I went back behind my house, jumped the fence and went to the weeds where I had stashed the amp. To my astonishment, it was gone! I rechecked my steps and the weeds where I hid the amp had been discovered and someone had taken the amp. For days, I pondered what could have happened. The weeds were still there and had not been cut.

It was not until years later that I found out that a kid, who lived in one of the row of houses facing 24th Street, was looking out his back window and saw me hide the amp. He then took the amp home the same day. So, in the end, we did not have any of the equipment, but we did learn something important, you must work hard for what you want from life, not steal it. Howell, Calvin, Telephone Interview with Chuck Miller, (11 Jan. 09), Orlando, Florida. [xiii]

Developing the Right Attitude

I later tried to instill in these young men the importance of honor and confidence as well as skills in musical performance, *vital lessons they would use when they and other groups from the Boys Club would have to be in competition with more polished musical groups in the city of Omaha.*

I could feel the talent in these young men. Many who were angry, hungry and doing mild drugs were ready to take on new challenges and head in a different direction. When you are teaching students who are hungry for knowledge and ready for a change, there is a feeling that comes over you that is hard to explain. That's something I will never forget.

After going to court with these young men, and after hearing the Judge enlighten them as to what would happened if they ever returned to her court room again, they were ordered by the court to study music with me at The Gene Eppley North Omaha Boys Club.

Photo courtesy of Chuck Miller

Chuck Miller, University of Nebraska Graduate.

These young men families were nothing like the family on the TV Show, "I Love Lucy", where the father always comes home from work, greeting the Mom with the famous slogan, "Honey I'm home".

This is a picture of a positive family; someone who share precious moments at meal times, and who have interesting day to day experiences to talk about just before retiring at bed time.

The Boys Club replaced the student's negative home atmosphere with a positive home atmosphere by greeting them with a nice hello, a smile and many times a great big hug when they came in the door.

No matter what department a member went into, the staffs made them feel special. Each male staff member became a father figure and each female staff member became a mother figure.

<u>This was the ingredient of our success</u>. We made the members want to come back each and every day. They found love, peace, joy and happiness in our presence. This concept proved that children lives are improved when they are in a loving relationship with others.

One of the things that helped me change my character and reach my goals in life was the following statement by author, Denis Waitley: "<u>It's not who you are that holds you back; it's who you think you are not</u>." These are the words that echoed in my mind every time I thought about the positive changes that were made in my life. Understanding this phrase and acting upon a few principals increased my self-esteem, improved my self-image and much more. I knew that if this worked for me it could very well work for these young men and young women. I felt in my heart that everybody has a potential to be successful; you just need a plan. Following is the concept we used in the music program at The North Omaha Boys Club with our at-risk youth. We concentrated on 10 qualities of a Total Winner designed by Dr. Waitley to develop positive characters in the lives of our young future musicians.

In a Progress Guide, author Denis E. Waitley, Ph.D. states:

lL

Everybody has the potential to make things better in their lives but many don't take advantage of the principals that are available. In the same way that scientists have established that we use less than 3% of our brain capacity, most of us use less than 3% of our potential for success in our lives.

Photo courtesy of Chuck Miller

<u>*Boys Club Drummer, Gary Williams.*</u>

In recent years, behavioral scientists have proven over and over again that most people have a potential for success that is almost never used. For example: Before the start of the school year, Dr. Prescott Lecky told a group of teachers that they would be teaching the brightest group of students in the school.

Actually, the students were chosen at random from the school's population. But by the end of the year, all of the

78

students were doing brilliant work, and the teachers were saying how wonderful these 'bright' students were to teach.

Photo courtesy of Chuck Miller

Boys Club young Musicians.

By making the teachers believe the students were exceptional, they treated them as exceptional. Because of the way the teachers treated them, the students also came to believe that they were gifted. The result was that the students performed like exceptionally gifted children.

This double-blind experiment proved beyond a shadow of a doubt that the power of thought has an affect on our performance. By duplicating this experiment time and time again, scientists have proved conclusively that nearly everyone has a potential for achievement that usually remains unused.

There were (**five attitude qualities**) and (**five action qualities**) used to help our young musicians change their behavior.

Photo courtesy of Chuck Miller

Boys Club Musicians: Rodney Jones, Curtis Cross, Frantz Harper and Adolph Williams.

The first **attitude quality** we used to develop the characters of our young musicians was the quality of:

1.   *Positive Self-Expectancy.* This is where we taught the students, the concept, *that in order for them to become an achiever at music or at any other activity they chose to pursue in life; they would have to first expect good things to happen to them.* After many of the rehearsals, I can still remember some of the students saying: "We played good today Chuck. But we'll play even better tomorrow.*" Now, when a student makes comments such as this, this is using Positive Self-Expectancy at its best.*

Photo courtesy of Chuck Miller

Boys Club Bass Player, Stanley Tribble.

2. <u>Positive Self-Motivation</u> was the **action quality** they learned. This quality reminded them that no one ever wins without motivation. We taught them the two greatest motivating powers in life and how to use them: *(1) their self-expectant personal and world view, and (2) their awareness that, while fear and desire are among the greatest motivators, fear is destructive while desire leads to achievement, success and happiness. With this concept in mind, they begin to focus their thinking on the rewards of success and actively tune out their fears of failure. We taught them that winners say, "I want to ... and I can do it ... and I will!" But Losers say, "I have to ... and I can't."*

Photo courtesy of Chuck Miller

Boys Club Musicians: **Row one**: Lois McMorris. Row two, left to right: Leonard Harris, and Chuck Miller. Row three, left to right: Garie Crowder and Bobby Griffo.

3.   The third **attitude quality** we used was called *Positive Self-Image. We taught the students that they had to want something so bad that they could taste it! This is the kind of desire they had to acquire in order to become successful. In other words, they had to become hungry for what ever they wanted out of life. As a new winner in life, they had to say to them selves over and over: "I can see myself changing now, I'm growing, I'm achieving and I'm winning."*

Photo courtesy of Chuck Miller

<u>Boys Club Saxophone Player:</u> Hank Thomas.

4.   I advised the musicians that, if they were going to become winners in life, they had to learn something about the fourth **action quality**, which was *Positive Self-Direction. Here they needed to have clearly defined game plans and purposes for their lives. They needed to know where they were going every day, every month, and every year. Their objectives should range all the way from lifetime goals to daily priorities. And when they are not actively pursuing their goals, they are thinking about them-hard! As winners they begin to say: "I have a plan to make it happen. I'll do what is necessary to get what I want."*

5.   The fifth **attitude quality** we talked about was *Positive Self-Control. They learned that they had to take full responsibility for everything that happens in their lives. They learned how to set priorities. They had to become self directed and learn how to plan their goals and break them down into*

daily priorities. As winners, they begin to say: "I take the credit or the blame for my performance."

6.   The sixth **action quality** was _Positive Self-Discipline_. This is where we taught the musicians how to practice techniques for winning in their minds before they got to the real situation. Here they mastered the art of simulation. Their self-talk became: "of course I can do it! I've practiced it mentally a thousand times."

7.   The next **attitude quality** we taught them was about _Positive Self-Esteem_. This quality taught the students that they were unique human beings. Recognizing their uniqueness, they developed and maintained their own high standards. They begin to accept themselves as imperfect, changing, growing, worthwhile individuals. Their self-talk became: "I do things well because I'm that type of person."

8.   The eighth **action quality** was _Positive Self-Dimension_. In mastering this quality, they had to learn to see themselves through the eyes of others. This taught them how to feel as one with nature and the universe. And they learned to be aware of time – their opportunity to learn from the past, plan for the future, and live as fully as possible in the present. They learned to create other winners without exploiting them. They begin to practice the Double-winning attitude: "If I help you win, then I win." You could see examples of them using this quality by the way they would help each other learn various aspects of music performance. They literally worked together with ease.

9.   The ninth **attitude quality** was _Positive Self-Awareness_. Here they had to learn who they were, what they believed in and figure out where they wanted to go. They also had to learn to live up to their goals and values that they had set for themselves. After mastering this quality, their self – talk

became: "I know who I am, I know where I am coming from, and I know where I am going."

10. The tenth and final **action quality** we taught the musicians was *Positive Self-Projection*. *Here they learned how to project their attitudes and ideas through everything they did. This helped them to become total winners in everything they were involved in.* Denis E. Waitley, Ph.D. (The Psychology of Winning), paraphrased.[xiv]

⅃

There have been some research on the affect music has had and is having on re-organizing the behavior of at-risk youths in our society. In a research conducted by Professor David Teachout, a professor at the University of North Carolina at Greensboro, various findings through the years revealed the following:

ᘝ

In 1960 (Bowman and Matthews') research revealed that, "Dropouts were involved in fewer extracurricular activities than were those who remained through graduation."

In 1986 (Ciborowski's) research revealed, that "Achieving students expressed more interest in life activities that involved music and drama than did underachieving students."

In 1987 (Acer's) research revealed that, "Integrating the study of language, music, drama, and dance for at-risk students could address many recommendations for juvenile delinquency programs."

In 1991 (West Virginia School Dropout Prevention Task Force's) research revealed that, "93% of dropouts were found to never participate in extracurricular activities."

In 1993 (Jenlink's) research revealed that, "Participation in a school's music program lessened students' feelings of alienation, promoted individual growth, and provided a common bond between home and school."

In 1999 (Taetle's) research revealed that, "Students not enrolled in fine arts electives had significantly higher absentee rates than those students with at least one fine art elective." Teachout, David (Can Music Education help At-Risk Students?).[xv]

These studies speak for themselves; they show that music plays an important part in the development of at-risk student's behavior and total growth. We were fortunate to have a Boys Club which taught behavior qualities that produced the results that were needed.

The staff was well trained in these techniques in one way or another; because we were required to attend workshops/meetings periodically which addressed these issues, a group is pictured below:

Photo courtesy of Chuck Miller

Club Meeting: Left to right across the table: Adolph Williams, Gary Williams, Charlie Williams, Charles Reynolds, David Bailey, Herbie Hancock and Judy.

Photo courtesy of Chuck Miller

Club Meeting: Left to right across the table: Herbie Hancock, Judy, Tom Davis, Adolph Williams and Gary Williams.

THE GREATEST BOYS CLUB STAFF

The Boys Club had a great staff. Some of our Executive Directors were: William R. Hinckley, Mary Dean Harvey, Thomas O. Davis and Fred W. Schott.

Photo courtesy of Margarette Ponds-Banks

William R. Hinckley, Executive Director.

Photo courtesy of Margarette Ponds-Banks

Thomas O. Davis, Executive Director.

An informative article appeared in the Omaha Star News Paper which highlights the career of Tom Davis, it can be seen below:

⌐

Former Boys & Girls Club Executive Honored

Orlando, Fla. – Thomas O. Davis, former executive director of the Boys & Girls Clubs of Omaha was inducted into the Boys & Girls Clubs of America Masters & Mentors Academy at the organization's national conference in Orlando.

In 1999, Boys & Girls Clubs of America established the Masters & Mentors Academy. Induction into the academy is the highest recognition available to past or present Boys & Girls Club professionals. This honor is bestowed on those men and women who have contributed to the development of career professionals and to the advancement of the Boys & Girls Club movement.

Since the academy's inception, 19 Club Professionals of the Movement has been installed. Today, Davis was one of four professionals inducted into the Master & Mentors. Davis epitomizes the organization's belief that lessons are taught by example.

Davis began his Boys & Girls Club career in 1963 with the Boys & Girls Clubs of Omaha, then Boys Clubs of Omaha. First hired as a part-time office attendant, Davis held a number of positions, including service director and unit director, before serving as the club's second executive director until his retirement in 1996.

Davis has served on numerous national committees for Boys & Girls Clubs of America, including the National Certification Board, the Task Force on Health and the Human Resources Advisory Committee. Throughout his career, Davis was an active member of the Association of

Thomas O. Davis

Boys & Girls Club Professionals (ABGCP), serving as chairman of the Iowa/Nebraska Chapter and as national vice president.

In 1987, Davis was named the ABGCP's National Professional of the Year for his outstanding service and dedication, and he has been honored with the Herman Prescott Award and the Bronze Keystone Award, among others.

Previous Masters & Mentors inductees with Omaha ties include William R. Hinckley (1999), the first executive director of the Boys & Girls Clubs of Omaha and A. Daniel A'Ossey (2001), a social recreation and camp director for the clubs.

Omaha's representation in the Masters & Mentors Academy – three inductees of the 23 inducted – is a testimony to the support the community has given to the clubs over the years to work with Omaha's youth.

The Omaha Star, Vol. 65 – No. 12, Omaha, Nebraska, Thursday, May 15, 2003, front page.[xvi]

⌐

Some of the other Unit Directors were: Jon McWilliams, James Ramirez, Dwight Day, Fred Schott, Willie Bob Johnson, Walter L. Henderson, Edward Hayes and David Felici.

Photo courtesy of Margarette Ponds-Banks

Thomas O. Davis, Unit Director.

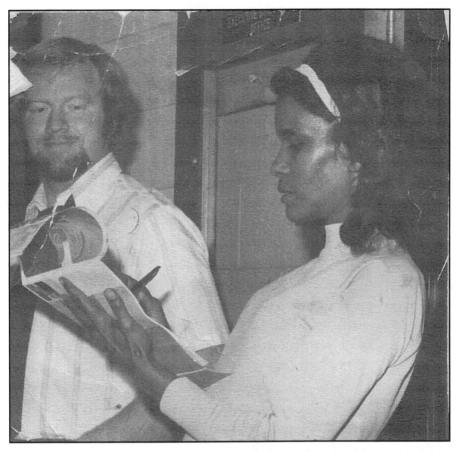

Photo courtesy of Margarette Ponds-Banks

Fred W. Schott, Unit Director,
pictured with him is Margarette Ponds-Banks, Secretary.

Chuck Miller

Photo courtesy of Margarette Ponds-Banks

Walter Henderson, Unit Director.

Photo courtesy of Margarette Ponds-Banks

Willie Bob Johnson, Aquatics Instructor and later Unit Director.

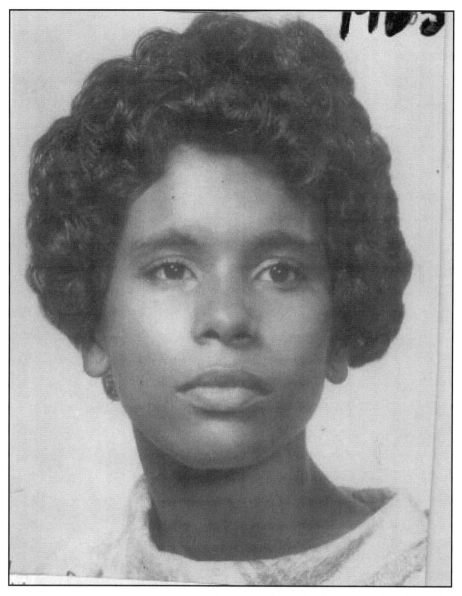

Photo courtesy of Margarette Ponds-Banks

Margarette Ponds-Banks, Librarian.

Some of the other Librarians were: Tom Hauser, Betty Hayes, Kevin Buckner, Charlene Duncan, and Karen Plummer (1963).

Photo courtesy of Chuck Miller

Left to right: Fred Schott, unidentified staff member, Alvin "Big Al" Lowe, and Charlene Dunkin.

Photo courtesy of Margarette Ponds-Banks

Dwight Day, Arts & Craft and later Unit Director.

Photo courtesy of Margarette Pond-Banks

Ike Snell, Unit Director.

Photo courtesy of Lonnie McIntosh

Alvin "Big Al" Lowe, Aquatics and Lonnie "Mr. Mack" McIntosh, Physical Education.

Photo courtesy of Lonnie McIntosh

Dennis "Tree" Forest.

A TYPICAL DAY AT THE CLUB

Photo courtesy of Lonnie McIntosh

A typical day for Boys Club members could involve many activities. One begins by entering through the front door and presenting an I.D. card to the attendant. From there, a whole new array of experiences was available.

IL

The late Calvin Howell:

"The North Omaha Boy's Club was a good walk from where we lived but, in those days, you didn't even think twice about walking a couple of miles or more in one direction to get to where you wanted to go. Plus, the Boy's Club had a kitchen that served lunch each day or a dinner meal.

We always were hungry and would dread not getting there in time before the food ran out, which most days, it usually did, especially when the cook made one of our favorite meals, like crab meat casserole. Man that dish would hardly last an hour and we would line up like little solders with tin plates in our hands. Only, we did not have tin plates, we had meal tickets.

To get meal tickets, you had to look poor, actually be poor, or know somebody who was poor, which was not hard to do in either case. There was however, a nice lady in the front office that would give us tickets when we could not afford the $0.25 to buy one, (which was most of the time). I forget her name but I'm sure many of my friends would remember her. Margarette comes to mind, but I'm not sure.

Dino and I loved Shop, loved to play pool, loved to play ping-pong, loved photography (which came later) and loved to bowl, when the bowling lane was put into the "new building". I also loved to swim and dive. For a while, I held several swim records for butterfly and breathe stroke and was on the swim team.

In fact, there were days when we would go through the locker room, which was guarded by "big AL", fake taking a shower and run and jump into the pool where the guy in charge was "Willie Bob" and later on, "Ken". I remember seeing Willie Bob work out in the gym to become a defensive back or something. He was a nice guy and everyone wanted to be in his Group Club.

Other swimming instructors were: Larry Podogil, Larry Garrett, Ken Glasser, Keith Lewis, Alvin Lowe and Wolf Man (The man with the wolf dog).

Playing pool at The Club was a challenge. We started out playing on a small table called a Bumper Pool table. Then we graduated to the 6 feet pool table where it was ok to call "Spaces" and move the cue from the rail. Our ultimate joys came when we moved to the intermediate area in The Club and were aloud to play on the full size pool and ping-pong tables. I was an avid ping-pong player who could beat the best.

We would all play, fight, laugh, eat, and run together. The tournaments were very competitive and it was a matter of pride to beat everyone in the eight ball tournament or the ping-pong tournament or whatever tournament was being run at the time. I honed my competitiveness at The North Omaha Boy's Club.

My children now seem to think that I learned everything I know at The Boy's club. Their thoughts are not that far from the truth when I stop to think about all the things I learned. In Sports I learned: football, baseball, basketball, swimming, bowling, archery, canoeing, boxing, pool, ping pong, table soccer and track & field. In Shop I learned: plastics, woodwork, ceramics, and photography. Our Social Recreation teacher was Dominick Giovinazzo. There were three Physical Education instructors, they were: Bill Stalnaker, Lonnie McIntosh, and a man from New Jersey name Bill. Mr. Mac (Lonnie McIntosh) was considered the greatest. Everyone wanted to be like him. There were staff members who were influenced by his character and his mannerism.

In Fine Arts I learned what has stayed with me the most, music. I can remember some of the names, Mr. Davis, Willie Bob, Big AL, Mr. Wright (Football coach), Chuck Miller (Music Instructor) and Jerry in the shop. Other workers in Arts and Crafts were: Dwight Day, Danny A'Ossey, and Bob Coby. Some of the music instructors before Chuck Miller were: Sister Mary Fortis, Andy, and Harold "Stemsy" Hunter.

Speaking of Chuck, I remember when they first started the new music program at Boy's Club. Back in those days, there would be an announcement over the loud speaker "In room such and such, there is going to be music instruction, anybody interested should go there by 4pm".

I remember nobody showed up but me. Everybody else went to some other things that were being announced at the same time. That was the deal. If you were interested in other things, you had choices. That was cool. Since I had just started playing bass, I wanted to see what was up in the "music room". I was a bit disappointed at first to find that I was the only one to show up.

But Chuck introduced himself to me and asked me my name and what instrument I played. At that time, I actually was in Jr. High and had switched from trumpet to low brass (baritone, trombone, and tuba) because those were the only "free instruments" at school.

If you wanted to continue with trumpet, you had to have your own horn. My parents did not know my passion for music at that time and got me a plastic trumpet with four keys for Christmas. I broke off the extra key and then the horn would not play at all. Then, I wished I had not broken off the 4th key.

It was Peyton Crossley who introduced me to music when I was in the Fourth Grade at Lothrop Elementary. He just said hey, want to get out of class and do something different? I said yes, so we went to "Band" and that's where I chose to pick up the trumpet, which I actually played for about 7 years. But, when I met Chuck, I was already getting into the bass I had just scored that summer.

I remember Chuck playing a little phonograph and listening to a tune bit by bit and writing out a chart of music to what he heard. Chuck was cool with his style and his ski cap that he used to wear all the time.

This blew me away and I wondered how he was able to do that. He would even put the various chords voicing on the score like Maj 7th, minor 7th or flat 5 etc. I wanted to know more about this "Theory". I found out later that Chuck was already working on his Master's Degree in Music at UNL.

Chuck became my mentor as I learned how to play jazz. To this day, I credit him with my early foundation and introduction to jazz. I'll never forget the ii – V – 1 progression or the 1 –VI – II – V – 1 progression he showed me back then. He also showed me a chording style on the piano that I still use today to chart out tunes with the bass line in the left hand and the right hand playing the chords." Howell, Calvin, Telephone Interview with Chuck Miller, (11 Jan. 09), Orlando, Florida[xvii].

Designing the Program and Music Curriculum

Although Calvin was not present in court with the other boys, the boys were his close friends. After they began attending music classes, I analyzed the degree of talent each student had, and came up with the idea to design a program with an original curriculum that would teach them the basic of music and drama and help them develop positive self-discipline skills at the same time. The program was constructed using three areas of concentrations: philosophy, instruction and support.

The music program encouraged the students to participate in the arts as an alternative to delinquent or negative activity. My philosophy was centered on the concept that all children can learn, no matter what their particular deficiencies in life were.

One example is of a student who faced these challenges was Matthew Rupert who had a speech impediment. As a young boy, Matthew went home from school many days in tears as a result of being ridicule by some of his peers because of his speech problem.

Every since his young days in grade school, Matthew dreamed of becoming a musician. He would beat on pots and pans, thinking of them as drums and other percussion instruments; he was in his own world. Although he had a speech impediment problem, he was determined not to let this problem stop him from reaching his goal, so he devised a plan of letting his friends speak for him when ever he needed them too. This worked very well while he was in school, however, when he first arrived and joined the Boys Club's Music Program, things changed drastically.

During our audition process, the other students were trying to speak for him as they often did at school, I immediately said no! He will have to speak for himself. No matter how hard it will be for us to understand him, he must speak for himself. He is shown in the photo below:

Photo courtesy of Chuck Miller

Drummer, Matthew Rupert.

This proved to be the best advice I could have given him. His self-image and esteem went to high levels and he became one of the most popular and admired students in the program. Even today, he is respected and loved by all of us. Not out of pity, but out of respect because he is able to do things just as well as anybody else.

The program's instruction method involved musical instruments and vocal performance, theory, history and analysis classes. Various representatives from community artists, nationally well known musicians and musical groups were also an active part of this concept.

Our classes increased youth's knowledge and skills, their interests in music activities, and their feelings of self worth. None of the participants displayed delinquent behavior during their involvement in the program. Students were involved in Group Clubs, Workshops and Jam Sessions, (the Club's daily performance assistance program.)

This program provided a challenging and inspiring after school alternative for many at-risk youth from the Omaha Public Schools, and served a critical need for Omaha children who would have had little or no access to musical training.

Our program was instrumental in developing the first coed instrumental and vocal groups in the Gene Eppley Boys Club System. As a result of my vision to add girls to the program, whether directly or indirectly, *we now have a combined Boys and Girls Club System*. After the curriculum was designed, I brought in a few old instruments and teaching/rehearsals began.

In order for the students to rehearse and function at their best, they had to be in top physical condition. I was fortunate to have a Physical Ed. Program laid out for me as part of the regular activities presented at the Boys Club.

The music students had the options of participating in football, baseball, basketball, swimming, bowling, archery, canoeing, boxing, pool, ping-pong, table soccer or track & field.

When it came time for band practice and theory classes, the students were physically and mentally prepared.

In designing the music curriculum, I used techniques from the Barry Gordy Motown Records Corporation. Gordy taught his entertainers modeling techniques, dance/choreography techniques, and he used people from various departments of the entertainment industry to select which songs they felt would become a hit record.

I used members from some of the Boys Club Bands to select new groups they felt were ready to go out into the community and perform. Each new group had to go through a *"Right of Passage"* program in order to be able to perform in public. In order to pass this program, a musician had to be able to play his major scales and know the formula for writing them out.

He or she would also have to learn how to sing and dance a little. Each student had to learn his/her part and be able to play it on the spot. They also had to have good grades in school and had to be a member of one of the Boys Club Group Clubs.

We always had plenty of musicians to help out where needed. If we needed a drummer, no problem, we could sometimes choose from five or six bands and find some good drummers. We would do the same for other instruments as needed.

One of our bands was organized using nothing but drummers. We accomplished this by teaching some of the drummers how to play other instruments. This proved to be very rewarding; many of these musicians became great performers as time passed.

6

FIRST THINGS FIRST

FIRST BOYS CLUB BAND, CONTACT BAND

The first band organized at the Club was called Contact, and later, my group Chazz. The late Calvin Howell remembers:

⌐

*When we formed our first band at The Club, I played bass, Dino Wright played guitar, Roderick Jones played keyboards and sung lead and background vocals, Gary Williams played drums and sung lead vocals, and Adolph Williams played trumpet. We called this first band **"CONTACT"**. It was born out of a group club we also had called "RAGDC" which was an acronym for all our first names: Roderick, Adolph, Gary, Dino, and Calvin.* Howell, Calvin, Telephone Interview with Chuck Miller, (11 Jan. 09), Orlando, Florida[xviii].

⌐

The first rehearsal was a complete disaster. No one knew how to play his instrument but everyone wanted to make music. The instruments we had were out of date and not very fun to play.

I remember one night the group played a dance for the general public at the Boys Club. We used the old jazz type music stand that Count Basie and Duke Ellington used whenever they performed. The young teens just laughed at the group and would not dance to our music. See the old jazz music stands below. Some of Contact musicians are pictured using those old music stands. See the photo below:

The North Omaha Boys Club Jazz Ensemble,
sitting behind old jazz type stands.

Left to right: Bryant McClinton Fisher bass, Dino Wright guitar, Richard
Thomas drums, Connie L. Miller alto saxophone,
Adolph Williams trumpet and Chuck Miller trumpet.

Gary Williams, Contact's drummer and lead singer
suggested that we get rid of the old outdated music stands and
stand up and play the way groups played on T.V. I must admit,
I was not too crazy about the idea (being a jazz buff), but it
proved to be the best move we could have made. People
started to dance to our music and everyone had a great time.
From that night onwards, the Contact group had made their
mark.

As time passed, members of the group Contact increased,
it's members now included: Gary Williams, drums; Tony Carter,
conga; Dino Wright, guitar; Calvin Howell, bass guitar; Adolph
Williams, trumpet; Raymond Moss, alto saxophone; Jimmy
Morse, percussion; Clyde Jacobs, percussion; and Roderick
Jones, organ.

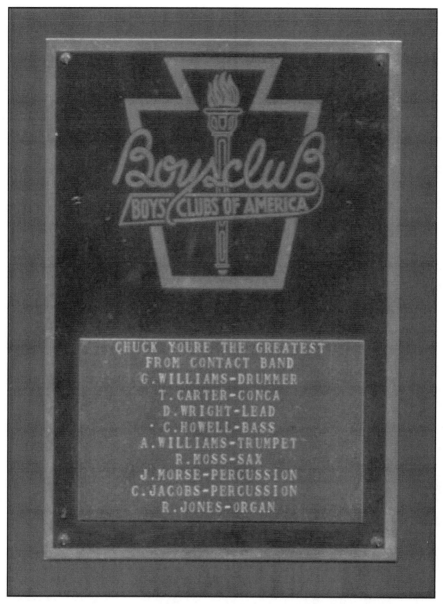

Photo courtesy of Chuck Miller

A Plaque from Contact Band to me, 1975.

<u>Names on the plaque, top to bottom</u>: Gary Williams, Tony Carter, Dino Wright, Calvin Howell, Adolph Williams, Raymond Moss, Jimmy Morse, Clyde Jacobs and Rodney Jones.

Within a short time, this group developed and became more successful than anyone thought possible. Half of my mission had been accomplished. I had shinned a light and brought hope into the lives of a few music personalities but more had to be done. More groups had to be organized and efforts had to be made to make The Club into *a coed atmosphere*, a feat that was unheard of during the seventies.

This was a powerful move on my behalf. Many of the Boys Clubs in New York and other major cities had not made that move during this time. One of the Corporate Boys Clubs from the New York area visited The Club to check out our program and invited me to write a new theme song for the National Boys Clubs of America. This was an honor and a first for me.

FIRST TIME EVENTS FOR ME

I have always been in positions to be first in accomplishing things. I was first to wear cap guns to school while in the third through fourth grades. Four other students and I patterned ourselves after Warner Brothers Cowboys (characters from the Warner Brother T.V. Shows) and wore cap guns, a white shirt, a Cowboy string tie and blue jeans to school each Friday, a feat no student should dare do today, because things have really changed.

I was the first in my school to write a musical composition and have it performed by our high school friends. I was the first of five siblings to attend a four-year university and the first African American student to graduate from the Music Department from The University of Nebraska at Omaha, (formally, OU).

I was also the first one in my immediate family to publish a book, record a major CD, travel the US with a major recording group (The Fabulous Rhinestones from New York City), be inducted into the McRae High School Hall of Fame in Prescott, Arkansas and the Black Music Hall of Fame in Omaha, Nebraska and the first to be Ordained as a Deacon.

First time performing and teaching opportunities at U.N.O.

Later in 1975, I begin working hard to finish my Under Graduate work in music at U.N.O. Things really begin to look good. I was able to perform with the U.N.O. Jazz Ensemble, which this time featured internationally known jazz trumpeter Clark Terry. It really felt great, standing up there in front of the band and playing a jazz solo with my trumpet. I was not a bit intimidated by Terry; I just felt we all had to do the best we could do.

Things worked out great for me. I was very much into the playing style of Miles David, Freddy Hubbard and Blue Mitchell, which gave me enough material to develop my solos. You can see me in the photo below as we performed the Miles Davis tune, "Miles Stones."

The University of Nebraska Jazz Ensemble

Photo courtesy of The Metro News Paper

Clark Terry and The University of Nebraska Jazz Ensemble, 1975.

From left to right: Eddie Russo, trombone, Clark Terry, trumpet, Steve Digert, tenor saxophone, and Chuck Miller take a solo on trumpet.

The University of Nebraska Soul Choir

Still armed with the desire to perform in the jazz vernacular, despite what I was advised by the Music Department Head, I continued practicing jazz and later I taught a class in jazz improvisation through the Black Studies Department by way of the Soul Gospel Choir under the direction of Ms. Alene Carter.

This was not a jazz choir but it did offer me a chance to play my trumpet in the gospel style. This was new to me and I enjoyed playing this style very much. I am pictured with the Soul Gospel Choir below:

Photo courtesy of Chuck Miller

University of Nebraska Soul Gospel Choir, 1975.

Standing at the front is our Director Alene Carter; I am standing to her left holding the trumpet. In addition to playing trumpet, I also sung tenor in this choir.

First to present a classical/jazz recital

I later became the first African American student to present a classical and jazz recital and the first to receive (as stated earlier) the Bachelors of Music Degree from UNO's Music Department. This was an exciting moment for me. See my advertising flyer below:

Photo courtesy of Chuck Miller

Chuck Miller's Classical/Jazz Senior Recital, 1975.

Chuck Miller, trumpet, Holly Nielson, accompanist and The Cliff Dudley Quartet, with Cliff Dudley, trombone; Jeanne Rogers, organ; Basie Givens, bass and Razz Rae, drums. The first classical and jazz combined recital of this kind ever held at UNO.

Again, this was a great moment for me. I became the first to perform both classical and jazz repertoire at a UNO music recital. The University had finally opened up and accepted a new genre of music in the Music Department.

The selections I performed in the classical genre were: *Largo and Allegro by George Friedrich Handel*, arranged by Fitzgerald; *Prayer of Saint Gregory* by Alan Hovhaness; and *Suit for Trumpet and Piano* by Arthur Frackenpohl.

Some of the jazz selections were as follows: *By the Time I Get to Phoenix* by Glen Campbell, an artist I remembers seeing perform in a small night club in Delight, Arkansas while I was doing one niters with my high school combo, The Moonlighters; and *Silver's Serenade* by Horace Silver.

My accomplishments while attending The University of Nebraska at Omaha have taken me into many new adventures and have helped me shape the lives of many. While our first Boys Club's group Contact continued to develop, there were other groups developing and performing in the city. I even organized my own group, I called it Chazz, more on this group later.

7

GROWTH OF THE MUSIC DEPARTMENT

NEW DEVELOPING GROUPS

Chazz Band

1975 was the year of Disco talk and bell-bottoms. My next group Chazz had both. We wore bell-bottom pants and we were up on the latest Disco talk. While Chazz was performing for the Mahogany Mannequin Review at Mr. G's Lounge, The group Chocolate City was performing at The Playpen and Walt's Bar. Bob Rogers' Lounge, Stage 2, The Champion Bar, The Wild Cherry, Image 90, Dingo's, The Showcase and The Beef Barron featured some of Omaha's top musicians.

It seemed as though everybody was in town: Mason and Gaylond Prince, Roy Givens, Rachetta Wilson, Worley Fowler, Jerry Suiter, Gerald Holts, Calvin Keys and Buddy Miles all had engagements somewhere in town. Omaha was a busy place.

The DJ's were busy also. The Showcase had Don "The Gray Ghost of Soul", Sweet Jay Ray was at the Universe of Love, Mr. Z was at The Tally Ho and Ken Collins was at Mr. G's Lounge.

A nice comment about the group Chazz appeared in the December, 1975 Inner City News (And Entertainment Guide), see the comment below:

⌐

A new Omaha Area soul group made their debut the same evening (as the Mahogany Mannequin Review) and Chazz is sure to be one of the better bands to emerge from the Omaha scene. Congratulations to Chuck Miller for organizing a well put-together group. Inner City News, Week of December 1975.[xix]

⌐

Chazz was a New Rock/Jazz group, which stayed quite busy. The group is shown in the photo below:

Photo courtesy of Chuck Miller

Omaha New Rock/Jazz Group "Chazz", 1975.

From left to right, back row: Bobby Griffo, tenor saxophone; Sam Singleton, vocals; Leonard Harris, organ; Lois McMorris, guitar; unidentified percussionist. From left to right, front row: Ray, drums; Chuck Miller, trumpet and vocals; and Garie Crowder, bass.

A New Contact Band

In 1976, as Television music video programs improved, many bands used females to compliment their all male groups. This intrigued me very much. I therefore got the idea to add females to one of our groups and Robin Jones was brought in to play trumpet with Adolph Williams in the group Contact. What a player she was. She could play high, low, in the middle and had a sweet tone. Not only could she play well but also she was a beautiful young lady with a nice Afro. The late Calvin Howell remembers details about this group:

L

We all lived within a few blocks from each other on Evans Street. There were Dino Wright, Adolph Williams, Roderick Jones, Gary Williams, Eli McCrarey, Robin Jones and myself. There always has to be a girl involved. I remember Robin when she was this little pretty girl who lived over on Pratt Street. She had great hair and a chocolate skin tone as well as good features on her face. I sort of liked her too. But, she ended up dating Adolph for several years.

I lived at 2415 Evans Street and Dino lived across the street at 2428 Evans Street. Adolph lived one block away to the north on Pratt Street while Roderick lived about three blocks down between Pratt and Evans Street. Gary lived the furthest away on Bristol Street.

All of us went to Lothrop Elementary School where we played together just about every day. We were very close friends who hung out and ate together over at each other's houses all the time. After school, we would all wind up at The North Omaha Boy's Club.

We all rode our bicycles to the Club and mine was the worst. We could not afford to buy a new one because my father was in the Service overseas, and things were very tough on my family. Someone finally stole my bicycle and I had to walk the alley's looking for parts. Sometimes I would borrow parts, or trade for parts to make up a bicycle.

One time, after I fixed my bicycle; my friends and I rode the bicycle trails over in Carter Lake, Iowa; we ended up in an all white neighborhood where they did not take kindly to blacks at all. A crowd of whites chased Dino, Darryl, Roderick, Barry, and a couple of other friends and me on our bikes.

My bicycle broke down as usual, the bearings on my sprocket were popping out and falling all over the ground, so I had to stop and I got surrounded. Thanks to my gift of gab, I talked myself out of a beating [fight], (as I would not have gone down easy) and Dino was the only one of my friends who even looked back or slowed down as the mob of white kids surrounded me. Dino was on his 10-speed. All my other friends kept riding and would not stop to help. Man, they high tailed it out! High tailed it to safety, back to the bicycle trails.

One summer, Dino and I made a deal that the first one to earn enough money would buy a guitar and the other one had to buy a bass so we could start a band. Dino was better than I was at saving, so he became the guitarist and I became the bassist.

My hopes of becoming a guitarist ended as a result of this one deal. Funny thing is, however, I was the one who had Jimmy Hendrix posters in my room from The Woodstock Festival. But Dino was more refined and was checking out Al Dimiola and this made his desire of becoming a guitarist stronger than mine.

It was Dino who let me listen to bassist Stanley Clarke's "School Days" and man that blew me away. Hearing someone play a bass like that influenced me a great deal. So, we took our instruments to the Boys Club when we heard that they were going to start a music program department.

Participating in this music program would cut into our fishing time, as we loved to go fishing for carp, bullheads or blue gills or whatever was biting every chance we got, but it *was well worth it. This new group Contact with the addition of Robin Jones was something special.* Howell, Calvin, Telephone Interview with Chuck Miller, (11 Jan. 09), Orlando, Florida[xx].

⅃

See the new group in the photo below:

Photo courtesy of Chuck Miller

New Horn Section Joins Contact Band, 1976.

Left to right: Dino Wright guitar; Gary Williams drums; Robin Jones trumpet; Eli McCreary trumpet; Greg Lawson alto saxophone; Jimmy Morse percussion; and Calvin Howell bass; Adolph Williams, trumpet; Clyde Jacobs, percussion and Roderick Jones, keyboards; not pictured.

Photo courtesy of Chuck Miller

Contact Band, 1976.

Left to right: Roderick Jones keyboards; Gary Williams drums; Robin Jones trumpet; Adolph Williams trumpet; Eli McCreary trumpet; Greg Lawson alto saxophone; Dino Wright guitar; Jimmy Morse percussion; and Calvin Howell bass; and not pictured, Clyde Jacobs, percussion.

Calvin continues:

𝕃

There was also a younger group of guys who were coming up behind us that took the name of Jam Squad, more on them later. I seem to recall that the Contact Band actually used that name for a little while before taking on the name Contact, because when we did the talent show at Horace Mann, we used the name Jam Squad.

With this band, we entered our first talent show at Horace Mann Jr. High. I can remember we played Mr. Magic, Do it till

Your Satisfied, and "Ain't No Sunshine When She's Gone", and "That's the Way I Like It" by KC and the Sunshine Band. I can't remember if we won or not but we sure had fun and all our friends and families were there to cheer us on.

I recall that we had the most makeshift equipment you can imagine since we could not afford good amps. We made the bass cabinet I was using from parts we could dig up and we borrowed the GK PA amp head from the Boy's Club to power it. We were a young band on the rise; but without equipment to help us sound good. It was all heart. Howell, Calvin, Telephone Interview with Chuck Miller, (11 Jan. 09), Orlando, Florida.[xxi]

It was now 1977 and the group Contact was on the move. With a few personnel changes and the group performed on KMTV Channel 3 Black on Black Show with host, the late legendary saxophonist Preston Love. The show was taped on October 30, 1977 and aired on November 1, 1977.

Photo courtesy of Chuck Miller

Preston Love with the Classic Contact Band, 1977.

Left to right: Charlie Williams alto saxophone, Greg Lawson alto saxophone, Robin Jones trumpet, Adolph Williams trumpet,

Gary Williams vocals & drums, and Preston Love host. Roderick Jones keyboards, Jimmy Morse percussion and Greg Bowie bass not pictured.

Photo courtesy of Chuck Miller

The Entire Classic Contact Band, 1977.

Left to right: Roderick Jones keyboards, Jimmy Morse percussion, Charlie Williams alto saxophone, Greg Lawson alto saxophone, Robin Jones trumpet, Adolph Williams trumpet, Gary Williams vocals & drums, Greg Bowie bass.

Chuck Miller age 33, overseeing the taping of the T.V. Show with the Classic Contact Band, 1977.

I was sitting there on the set, with my arms folded, proud of the accomplishments of the Contact band. They had arrived! They could now perform as well as any group in the city. There was no stopping them now; they had come a long way from the court system.

Everyone was doing fine in the Boys Club's band and in their high school. Many of these young musicians became volunteer music teacher/helpers at the Club. It was great watching them share their talents with new band members. With this group, I could run any type of show production. They were able to set up the stage, run lightings, sound and handle costume design.

Alto Saxophonist Greg Lawson remembers the group this way:

IL

My greatest memories are from some of the gigs we played, and all the times we spent rehearsing there at the Boys Club and performing in public.

Here is how I became a part of the band. I was a sophomore at Tech High in 1976. I've always loved music and wanted to be a musician from the first time I saw Elvis Presley playing his guitar and singing when I was a small child. (There weren't many black musicians on T.V. back in those days), in fact I wanted to play the guitar.

When I joined my high school band, I was told they didn't use guitars. So, the band director basically handed me a clarinet and said, "This is your instrument now." So, to make a long story short, I learned to play the clarinet.

My good friend Gary Williams was the one who told me about the band that was starting at the Boys Club. I think I asked if they needed a clarinet player and he said they could probably use a saxophone player. Since the fingerings of the clarinet and sax were the same, I switched to sax.

My mom eventually rented a saxophone for me and I started showing up at band practices at the Boys Club. At that time it was just Gary Williams, Greg Bowie, Adolph Williams, Clyde Jacobs, Jimmy Morse, Robin Jones, Roderick Jones and I. The young great saxophonist Charlie Williams joined the group a short time later, and we got a lead guitar player whose name I don't remember.

My most memorable gig we played was the time we played on the T.V show "Black on Black". I remember playing a Bootsy Collins song called "The Pinocchio Theory". I'm sure we played a 2nd song, but I don't remember what it was. But shortly after appearing on that show I remember being at a party and having a girl ask me for my autograph. I thought it was kind of funny, but I gave her an autograph. I think that was the only time that had ever happened in my life.

Photo courtesy of Chuck Miller

Chuck Miller at age 33, performing with the Classic Contact Band, 1977.

Left to right: Charlie Williams alto saxophone, Greg Lawson alto saxophone, Robin Jones trumpet, Adolph Williams trumpet, Gary Williams vocals & drums, Chuck Miller (Our Producer) trumpet, Greg Bowie bass, Roderick Jones keyboards, and Jimmy Morse percussion; not pictured.

I also remember playing a talent show at Tech High. We played a song called "Slide", by a band named Slave. In the opening line of the song one of the band members introduces himself as "Drac" (short for Dracula we assumed).

He says "But I ain't gonna bite you though. I just want you to hang on." So we decided to adapt a Dracula theme for that show and we all wore black capes. My mother actually made them for us. I don't remember if we won the talent contest or not. That probably means we didn't. But anyway, we had a great time.

Another one of my most memorable gigs was when we played at the Boys Club. This event was open to the public. Members from my family were there. I think my mother; my aunt, my brother and my sisters were there to support me.

This was the only time they got to see me perform with the band Contact. In fact, I believe all of the band members had family there. This made the event very exciting. I believe "Love ETC" played that evening as well. I remember it as being almost like a battle of the bands. There was lots of discussion afterwards as to who was the better band. To my recollection the opinions were very mixed.

There was a rehearsal that sort of stands out in my mind too. We had been rehearsing pretty hard. I remember Chuck working a lot with Roderick, who was our keyboard player at the time.

Chuck also worked a lot with the horn section; trying to get the harmonies right. We had a great section at this time. I played alto saxophone, Charlie Williams played alto and Tenor saxophone, and Adolph Williams and Robin Jones played trumpet.

I remember Chuck took a break and actually left the band room. So, while the cats away the mice will play. We just started goofing around and someone suggested we play a song in slow motion. So we played "Brick House" in slow motion.

We were all moving very slow and playing the song very slowly. And the singers were singing in a really low voice trying to emulate a record or tape when you slow it down. It was hilarious.

We had lots of fun. Those are times that I will never forget. Of course Chuck Miller was our hero. Most of us knew very little about music. So, to us he was the master. We really appreciate that he took the time to teach us and guide us the way he did.

I will be 50 this year (2009) and I still enjoy playing and performing when I can. I've been teaching my boys how to play *and they enjoy it very much. Those were seeds that were planted back in my days at The Gene Eppley North Omaha Boys Club, and they have since paid off in making us what we have become. I really appreciate the Boys Club for having a program such as the one created by our mentor, Chuck Miller.* Lawson, Greg, Telephone Interview with Chuck Miller, (13 Jan. 09).[xxii]

Contact band began performing all around the city at various events. Besides performing for teen dances, talents shows, show wagons, and family parties, the group performed for more important functions.

New vocal competition

There was one other young lady who began singing with various groups in the club and man could she sing; her name was Bridgett Johnson. Bridgett had the kind of personality that could fit with any group or with any individual. She was talented, smart and was liked by all who met her. I could count on her to help with anything. She is pictured in the photo below:

Photo courtesy of Chuck Miller

Bridgett Johnson, performing with various Boys Club Band Members.

Left to right: Robin Jones trumpet, Gary Williams drums, Chuck Miller (Our Producer) trumpet, Bridgett Johnson vocals, Jimmy Morse, percussion and Greg Bowie bass.

The North Omaha Boys Club Jazz Ensemble

Once they performed at the Boys Club's national banquet, where representatives from all over the United States were present. For this occasion we formed The North Omaha Boys Club Jazz Ensemble.

This group performed music that was more suitable for adult clientele. Selections like Mr. Magic, Summer Time, Chameleon, Love, and the Blues were more appropriate. See their photo below:

Photo courtesy of Chuck Miller

The North Omaha Boys Club Jazz Ensemble, 1978.

This time standing without the old jazz type stands. Five from left:
Dino Wright, guitar; Connie L. Miller, alto saxophone and percussion; Richard Thomas, drums; Adolph Williams, trumpet; notice Michael Ware is added on percussion; and Bryant McClinton Fisher, bass.

By 1978, the Boy's Club music program had become more successful than anyone had dreamed. Within a year of its inception, the program attracted youth and adults of various races and cultures to participate.

The instrumental, vocal and dramatic interpretation of popular music was spread all over the Omaha area, and it influenced generations of musicians, dancers, DJ's and other professions, giving hope and directions to those in need.

Love E.T.C. Band

By 1979, musicians from all over the city joined The Club to receive a ray of hope from our program. One group was a group called "**Love ETC**". Members from this group included: Alan Gray, drums, Donna Jennings, percussion, Franz Harper, percussion, Teddy Reynolds, guitar, David Bailey, bass, Carol Fitzgerald, vocals and keyboards, William Huston, clarinet/saxophone, Curtis Cross, trumpet and Charles Reynolds, trumpet.

Photo courtesy of Chuck Miller

Love ETC Band, 1979.

David Bailey, bass; the late Carol Fitzgerald (in fir coat), vocals; and Teddy Reynolds (#76 on jersey), guitar.

129

I remember this group coming to the Club and watching the group Contact perform at one of their concerts. They just stood around looking at every move the band made. I could tell they wanted to train with us.

Finally after the concert was over, the bass player David Bailey approach me and asked me if I would consider letting the group study with me at the Club? Of course my answer was yes, come on in and join us.

SCHEDULING OF MUSIC CLASSES

I had a very full schedule. Since the Club was closed on Mondays, I used that time for preparation. Beginning on Tuesday afternoon, I taught private lessons from 1:30-2:00 p.m. From 2:00-2:30, beginning drums music reading class and drums & bugle corps preparation. At 3:00, I had private lessons again, from 4:00-4:30, beginning guitar lessons, 4:30-5:00, more private lessons, from 5:30-6:30, bass class, and finally at 7:30, I taught music theory and improvisation classes to adults and young adults. As you can see, there was no time left to rehearse the bands.

Wednesdays were reserved for rehearsing all of the bands. The times were pretty much the same. I began my teachings at 1:30 with private lessons. Next at 2:00-2:30 the ETC band rehearsed, followed by Comfort band, Quality band, Tempo band and Contact band, more on them later. This same schedule continued on Fridays and Saturdays, with one exception, ETC band didn't rehearse on Saturdays.

We ran a tight ship. Each band rehearsal began with prayer and goal setting. After that was in order, we choose a song to work on. Everyone was given a recording of the song and a copy of the arrangement I wrote especially for each individual musician. The song was then taken home, listened too and brought back to rehearsal ready to be perfected.

Not only was the instrumental music perfected, they also had to work very hard to perfect dance routines, stage presence and vocal music harmony and lead parts. One of the good things about our program is that each individual musician brought to the band something special. Talent flourished throughout all of the musicians. This was a time of miraculous growth on all of our part. We had a great time learning together.

THE 4TH ANNUAL SWEETHEART PAGEANT & DANCE

After Robin Jones was successful entered into the Contact group, I later begin to bring more and more young ladies into the Club's music program. I wanted the girls to be able to display their talents in more ways than just in bands; therefore I organized a "Sweetheart Pageant." In order to be a contestant a young lady had to be a relative of someone who worked at the Boys Club. This event became very popular at the Club. Following are highlights from news paper clippings and photos from a local Television program called "Black on Black:"

Fourth Annual Sweetheart Pageant and Dance

4th Annual Sweetheart Winner, Miss Karman Booker.

Friday evening, February 8th, 1980, was an evening that will be remembered very distinctly by all who viewed and participated in the North Omaha Gene Eppley Boys' Clubs 4th Annual Sweetheart Pageant and Dance. One who will treasure that evening for a long time is Miss Karmen Booker, this year's pageant winner.

After months of preparation, Mr. Chuck Miller, North Omaha Boys' Club Cultural Arts Director, put all the pieces together. He and staff built the whole pageant from scratch. This included the program, script, stage, sound, lights, videotape, television coverage, just to name a few.

The pageant began with Mr. Ronald Victor Parker, this year's master of ceremonies, welcoming everyone to the pageant. He then introduced Mrs. Helen Pinkard who sang, rather beautifully the Black National Anthem. Most all will agree that there aren't too many following acts as well performed as Mrs. Pinkard's, but this year's Sweetheart Contestants kept everyone well entertained.

This year's Sweetheart Pageant Contestants were Miss Arnita Harvey, Miss Bridget Johnson, Miss Karmen Booker, Miss Nikki Jacobs, Miss Paula Lollar, Miss Lisa Carroll, Miss Joy Lewis, and Miss De Edra Givins. The contestants were judged on their talent, poise, modeling and projecting abilities.

The panel of judges were Shirley Moore, proprietor of "California Limited Boutique", which also supplied some of the pageants wardrobe; Bob Runnels KMTV 3 which televised a portion of the pageant on the evening news. And Glenda Rhodes, a Union Pacific employee.

During a short intermission a talented group consisting of five beautiful young ladies and one young gentleman, (Fire & Force), entertained the audience. As the judges tallied the votes, Clifford Moore sang the pageant's theme song "Reaching for the Sky". The time has finally arrived to an-

(Continued on Page 9)

Fourth Annual Sweetheart Pageant and Dance

From left, Joy Lewis, Lisa Carroll, Paula Lollar, Nikki Jacobs, Deëidra Givens, Karmen Booker, Bridget Johnson and Armita Harvey.

From left, standing, Paula Lollar, 2nd Runner-up; Joy Lewis, 1st Runner-up and seating is Winners Karman Booker.

From left, Judges Glenda Rhodes, Bob Runnels and Shirley Moore.

Photo courtesy of The Omaha Star News Paper

Photo courtesy of Chuck Miller

The 1980 North Omaha Boys Club Sweetheart Pageant winner:

Karmen Booker.

Sweetheart Pageant's Master of Ceremonies: Ronald Parker. Sitting in the rear in charge of lighting is the late James Drue Benson who designed and built the Run-way slighted stage.

Photo courtesy of Chuck Miller

Clifford Moore sings the Pageant's theme song: "Reaching for the Sky" while Master of Ceremonies Ronald Parker and stage designer and builder the late James Drue Benson is in the rear.

To showcase the talents of these new groups, I organized new performances at talents shows, dances, pageants, and drug education concerts, battle of the bands, show-wagon and more television appearances. *There was no stopping us now, because we were on the move.*

8

IT'S MY TURN

After the great success of Contact, other individuals wanted to join the program. However, before they were allowed to join a group, they had to stand by the large window of the band room and watch Contact band as they rehearsed. I used this technique to help entering student get a feel of what to expect whenever they got a chance to join the program.

They received an early chance to see the discipline and endurance it would take for them to reach their goals in the program. This became a *right of passage* for all entering new band members. Sometimes individuals would stand by the window for months waiting their turn to study in our program.

THE OTHER BANDS

Tempo Band

The next group to come into fruition was called "**TEMPO**." This group was very special to me because these were my babies. The youngest in the group was 8 years old; his name was Timmy Kilgore. Timmy played keyboards and he learned everything I showed him. This was a phenomenal thing. This little guy could literally play back quickly the chords and melodies I would show him. I had never witnessed anything like it. He was the most gifted young musician I had seen during this time.

Another youngster who was equally as talented as young Kilgore was guitarist Clarence Nichols. Clarence was a year older than Timmy but had the same desire to learn his instrument. I started teaching him at 9 years old and he learned everything

I taught him. It seems as though the guitar was made for him; he adapted so easily to it. I later used Clarence in one of my professional groups, more on that later.

Kenny Brown, the group's drummer was a little more experienced because of his age. He was about 12 years old at the time. A very smooth drummer with a great attitude; nothing could make him loose his cool; he was the perfect student. You could count on Kenny to have his part before any of the other musicians. He was the type of drummer that watched the band to see exactly what needed to be done. Many drummers are to busy doing other things and is not as effective in leading the rhythm section the way Kenny did.

Another part of the rhythm section is the bass. Bryant McClinton Fisher filled this slot. I later used Bryant in the Master Chazz band. What a gifted young man, only 12 years old and destined for greatness. He could do it all. He could play jazz, rock, blues, R&B and funk. The great thing is he loved each style equally. He always laid down the foundation and not try to get in the way of the guitar player trying to solo all the times. He is the ideal player for any group. There will be more on him later.

My favorite instrument is the trumpet and Rodney Nichols became one of the best to study at the Club. Not only was he a dedicated student of the trumpet but he showed interest in playing the keyboards also. Rodney was the type of student that took pride in his performance. He would spend hours and hours perfecting his parts to make the group sound better. He had a great sound and could project his sound to the audience, which complemented the band greatly.

Our last talented musician was Jimmy Morris. Jimmy played alto saxophone and sung background vocals with the group. He had great stage presence and seemed to love performing in front of people. To watch him perform gave the audience a treat, something they would remember for quite some times. For an 11 year old, he could make that saxophone talk, what a great sound he had. The group is pictured below in one of their concerts:

Photo courtesy of Chuck Miller

Original/Classic Tempo Band in concert, 1976.

<u>Left to right, back row</u>: Timmy Kilgore, organ; Kenny Brown, drums; Clarence Nichols, guitar; Bryant McClinton Fisher, bass/vocals Left to right, front row: Rodney Nichols, trumpet, Jimmy Morris, alto saxophone and me on trumpet.

Photo courtesy of Chuck Miller

Original/Classic Tempo Band in concert, 1976.

Left to right, back row: Timmy Kilgore, organ not visible; Kenny Brown, drums; Clarence Nichols, guitar, Bryant McClinton Fisher, bass/vocals Left to right, front row: Rodney Nichols, trumpet; Jimmy Morris, alto saxophone and Chuck Miller, trumpet.

Some of the songs they played at their performances were: 1. Get Down Tonight, 2. That's The Way I Like It, 3. A Love of My Own, 4. Do It Any Way You Wanna, 5. Car Wash, 6. Get Up Off Of That Thing, 7. Play That Funky Music 8. Shake Your Booty, 9. Ain't No Sunshine When She's Gone, 10. Disco Dazz, 11. I'll Be Good To You, 12. Low Down, 13. Just To Be Close To You.

Tempo was a great young group who was equally as talented as any member of Contact or E.T.C. band. Only time would tell if they as individuals would become greater.

Jam Squad Band

The next group to form at the Club was a group called **"JAM SQUAD."** Each group worked hard to receive the success they received and Jam Squad was no exception. These fellows worked day and night trying to come up with new ideas for dance routines and song arrangements.

They had too because the competition was so strong. All of the groups including Contact and E.T.C., practiced at the same place, but at different times. Each group wanted to out do the other but in a friendly way. They would never talk negative about each other. Each band member was eagerly waiting a chance to substitute for another member in case someone couldn't make the rehearsal or a gig.

According to Thomas Wells, he and Stanley Tribble started this group. "It seemed we were the only two-student left that didn't have a group. So we asked Chuck if we could start our group and call it Jam Squad. I am not sure if Chuck really liked the name; however, he let us use it and made room for us to begin rehearsing, Thomas said." Recently in 2010, Thomas Wells was offered a position playing bass guitar in Lela Hathaway's group, they were to tour Japan. Due to prior commitments, Thomas was unable to accompany her. She used the bass player from the group Atlantic Star instead. However; the position is still opened for Thomas as soon as he is free from his commitments. Below is a photo of bassists Thomas Wells and a Boys Club friend Bryant Fisher. The two are participants in the upcoming documentary about North Omaha Boys Club Bands for the PBS Broadcasting Network for Public Television.

Photo courtesy of Branden T. Miller

From left to right*: Thomas Wells and Bryant McClinton Fisher.*

Members of this early Jam Squad group were: Roy Davenport, vocals, Stanley Robinson, vocals, Clarence Nichols, guitar, Thomas Wells, bass, Rodney Nichols, trumpet, Ronnie James, trumpet, Stanley Tribble, drums. This group performed at the Club and at various talent shows, show wagons and community dances.

Soon Jam Squad band added some new members to the group. The group now consisted of: Bobbie Hilliard, vocals; Roy Davenport, vocals; Robert Smith, vocals; Clarence Nichols, guitar; Stanley Tribble, bass; Rodney Nichols, keyboards; Ronnie James, Keyboards; and Andrea Stennis, drums. Noticed that Stanley Tribble is now playing bass, Andrea Stennis replaced Stanley Tribble on the drums, and Rodney Nichols and Ronnie James switched to playing keyboards. Rodney is pictured below receiving a lesson in keyboard playing from drummer/bass player Stanley Tribble:

Photo courtesy of Margarette Ponds-Banks

Left to right: *Stanley Tribble and Rodney Nichols.*

With this change in-group line-up, Jam Squad was now ready to compete with any group on the scene. This would include Contact, E.T.C. and any group from within the city of Omaha.

Through the course of time other band members included: Brian Holland, saxophone and background vocals; Daryl Beasley, bass and background vocals; Kenny Brown, drums/percussion; Tony Bailey, lead and background vocals/song writer; and Ronnie James became their sound technician/band business manager.

As time passed, and after many weeks of preparation, you could catch this group performing all over Omaha and a few out of town engagements. They once appeared on a show at Hannibal's Lounge with E.T.C., Destiny, Little Mack Murray and Square Biz and were able to hold their ground.

Jam Squad was a very polished group as were all of the groups who studied at the Club. Wherever they performed, they represented the Boys Club greatly. The group had new out-fits made and used intricate chorography dance routines that gave their performances pizzas. They opened concert for many international performing groups, one of these was a group called The Deele and BabyFace. The concert was held at the Auditorium Civic Center. The group is pictured below:

JAM SQUAD

P.O. BOX 11126
Omaha, NE 68111
(402) 551-0620

Rodney Nichols   Ronnie James

100% Jam   Music That Spreads

Photo courtesy of Terrance Bailey

Jam Squad, the Classic Group.

Left to right, row one: the late Roy Davenport, vocals; Robert Smith, vocals; left to right, row two: Tony Bailey, lead and background vocals/songwriter; David Bailey, bass/vocals/songwriter; Clarence Nichols, lead and rhythm guitar/songwriter; left to right, row three: Rodney Nichols, keyboards/songwriter/band leader; Kenny Brown, drums/percussion; Craig Franklin, keyboards/background vocals/songwriter; and not pictured, Ronny James, sound technician/band business manager.

Soon the group experienced some hard times and had to add some new personnel. However, they were determined nothing would stop them from keeping the band together and becoming the great band they knew they were destined to become. In the Omaha Star News, Gerald Evans wrote:

L

Jam Squad Band Omaha announces the signing of Daryl Beasley and the return of Bobby Hilliard. Daryl will perform duties as bass guitarist and vocalist and Robert will perform as lead and background vocalist. In making the announcement, Jam Squad's President, Roy Davenport says both individuals are strong additions to the group. "I don't think you'll find too many groups that work as hard as we do to perfect our sound and stage act, Roy says."

Jan Squad, a top-forty rhythm-and-blues band gaining wider recognition in the Omaha-Des Moines area triumphed over some difficult times last year that may have spelled the demise of other such groups. Just as we were placing the final touches on our act, we lost a capable bass player and singer. But not once did we consider breaking up," Roy says.

On the contrary, the situation forced the members to call on their skills as accomplished musicians and singers. "We just worked around the vacancy as best we could," he says. Keyboardist, Craig Franklin and Lead Guitarist, Clarence Nichols doubled, thus temporally filling the bass guitar responsibilities. "The doubling worked so well that only our loyal fans knew that we were missing an individual. Most importantly, we were fortunate to have kept our sound intact. "Roy adds. Doubling is a term applied to musicians who perform on two or more instruments.

Even though the band was "getting by" without a true bassist, Roy says Jam Squad was relentless in its search to fill the vacancy. Compounding the less than ideal situation, one of the group's key vocalists, Bobby Hilliard, departed with an illness which prevented him from performing for several weeks. "We wondered then if it was going to be possible to continue," Roy says," but we persevered."

Even without Bobby's strong vocals and a committed bassist, the group was able to carry on such engagements at the Elks Lodge, Bob Gibson's Spirits and Sustenance and Dreamers without difficulty. Admittedly," it looked pretty funny with two singers moving through our dance steps choreographed for three dancers. I'm also sure people in the audience, for which we have performed, had problems understanding what was going on as the musicians traded instruments between songs on stage.

As the group auditioned bass players, Roy says Daryl stood out among the others. "He has all the tools we need for the high-energy fast-paced show we give." Talks continued for more than a month before Jam Squad was able to land Daryl. Fortunately, Jam Squad's problems were ending long before Daryl joined the group. Bobby recovered sooner than expected from his illness and rejoined Jam Squad last December following a near three months absence.

Now at full strength, the band often compared with other well known recording stars, has over-come its biggest hurdles. "We are looking at 1986 with great optimism. Internally, we are saying this is the year for Jam Squad. We have all the tools, including a strong management base, talented personnel, professionalism and desire. These attributes can only mean success for Jam Squad for years to come.

"We are ready to show Omaha our new look and improved show as we continue striving to be a source of inspiration for younger musicians who will fill our shoes someday." Members in the band in the band include Robert Smith, lead and background vocals; Bobby Hilliard, lead and background vocals; Roy Davenport, lead and background vocals; Clarence Nichols, guitar; Rodney Nichols, keyboards; Craig Franklin, keyboards; Brian Holland, saxophone and background vocals; Andre Stennis, drums; Daryl Beasley, bass and background vocals; and Ronnie James, sound engineer. The Omaha Star, Gerald Evans.[xxiii]

⌐⌐

R-Style Band

Jam Squad later merged into a group called **R-Style**, a powerful R&B style group with great talent and command of the music. Many of the musicians from Jam Squad and E.T.C. remained in this new group. They have performed allover the Omaha area, Lincoln and beyond. They opened concerts for many international recording artists.

One of their largest performances was performing at the Riverfront for the annual Jazz and Blues Festival. The headliners included: Guitarist, Norman Brown; War and Jeff Lober of Summer Storm on keyboards. The Group is still active today. They are pictured below:

Photo courtesy of Terrance Bailey

R-Style

Left to right, row one: Robert Smith, vocals; the late Roy Davenport, vocals; left to right, row two: Terrance Bailey, guitar; Andrew Brookins, drums; David Bailey, bass; and Craig Franklin, keyboards.

Later, Jerry "Duke" Riggs replaced Brookins on drums, and Thomas Wells replaced Bailey on bass.

Comfort Band

Standing by the window next was a group of fellows who called themselves "COMFORT." Members of the group were: O.J. Pullin, Ronnie Hill, bongos; Michael Johnson, trumpet; and Richard Wair, alto saxophone. They would rehearse on Wednesday's and Friday's from 3:00 until 4:00 p.m. and from 4:00 until 5:00 p.m. on Saturdays. Soon others joined the group and became very successful, they are pictured below:

Photo courtesy of Chuck Miller

Comfort Band.

Left to right: Row one: Kevin Clemmons, vocals; the late Kelly Clemmons, vocals and flute; Alvin Lowe's niece, vocals; and Mario Cobino, vocals. Left to right: Row two: Eugene Hall, guitar.

This group was eagerly waiting their turn to join the program because when they joined, they were serious and ready to join the ranks. After many rehearsals, theory classes, workshops and in-house performances, they were ready to join the heavy weights.

On Friday June 10, 1977, Comfort shared the stage with Contact. They performed in a "School Is out Dance" which was packed with students from all over the city. The dance started at 9:00 p.m. and ended at 12:00 p.m.

Contact performed first. They performed the following selections: 1. Intro, 2. I'll Be Good to You, 3. A Love of Your Own, 5. Get up off That Thing, and 6. I Wish.

Next was Comfort's time to perform. They performed the following selections: 1. I Like It (Introduction), 2. Time is movin' on, 3. Brick House, 4. What's a Telephone Bill? 5. That's The Way I Like It, 6. Hollywood. This completed the first half of the dance. The DJ finished the night by spinning records.

Star Scope Jazz Ensemble

During this year of 1977 each band were doing great, therefore, I organized an adult group called "**THE STAR SCOPE JAZZ ENSEMBLE**." There is no photo available for this group. Members of the group were: Chuck Miller, trumpet; Dave Paulson, tenor saxophone; Kirk McKean, tenor saxophone; Hank Thomas, alto saxophone; Eddie Russo, trombone; Sherman Johnson, trombone; Benny Harris, bass; and Gary Williams, drums.

We were mostly a rehearsal group organized to experiment with learning jazz improvisation techniques and developing reading skills. There were some great young jazz musicians in this group. Many who went on to become very successful performers and teachers later in their careers.

High Fidelity Band

In July of 1978 the Gene Eppley North Omaha Boys Club added to its music department a new Disco-Soul performing group called "**High Fidelity**." The group was made up of both male and female members. Their names were: Colette Miller, age 12, vocals/trumpet; Cheryl Miller, age 13, vocals/trumpet; Connie Miller, age 15, vocals/alto saxophone; Timmy Kilgore, age 10, organ; Clarence Nichols, age 11, guitar; Delbert Tucker Moore, age 11, drums; and Tracy Rhone, age 12, bass.

Chuck Miller

High Fidelity Band Member, 1978.

Tracy Rhone, bass.

High Fidelity Horn Section with other Musicians, 1978.

Left to right, back row: Bryant McClinton Fisher, bass; Delbert Tucker Moore, drum; Clarence Nichols, guitar; Damien Turner, guitar; Left to right front row: Charles Reynolds vocals; Cheryl Miller, trumpet; Colette Miller, trumpet; and Connie Miller, alto saxophone.

Photo courtesy of Chuck Miller

High Fidelity Horn Section with me, their Dad.

Left to right front row: Colette Miller, organ; Connie Miller, alto saxophone; Cheryl Miller, trumpet; back row: Chuck Miller, trumpet.

Photo courtesy of The Metro News Paper

High Fidelity Horn Section.

Left to right front row: Colette Miller, trumpet; Connie Miller, alto saxophone; and Cheryl Miller, trumpet.

This group was very young and had a sound of its own; no doubt they went to great heights as they developed musically and spiritually. They later played for dances, talent shows and other special fun events at the Boys Club and the community. Many of these students became great performers, educators and business associates.

Quality Band

This next group was called "**QUALITY.**" Members of this group were some of the toughest students in the Club. These were junior high dropouts, gang members, and students who got into trouble most of the time. They were considered the worst of the crop. They were as follows: Steve Chatman, organ; Dave, bass/vocals; Orlando, guitar; Michael Tucker, drum; Robert Brown, trombone; and Dwayne Tucker, trumpet/vocals.

My vision was; any student can be helped; no matter what conditions their lives are in. I first realized that if these students took the time to stand by the window and watch the other students rehearse, they must have a desire to do the same. This was my key to understanding what was going on in their minds. These were kids who were tired of making mistakes, tired of goofing off and watching others succeed and making progress with their lives, while they failed. These kids wanted a change. Their involvement in the music program began with them joining one of the "group clubs" that was available. These clubs taught them how to respect others, self-discipline skills and the importance of being honest.

Armed with these new skills, the band was ready to begin musical training. I had each member write down goals they individually and as a group wanted to achieve. Next they had to do as all of the other students did, participate in some kind of sport event at the Club. There were many examples: football, basketball, track, swimming, plays ping-pong, pool or lift weights. I even recommended arts and crafts as a hobby.

As time passed some of the band members changed, this produced the classic Quality band. The band now consisted of

Mike Tucker, drums; Dwayne Tucker, trumpet; Robert Brown, trombone; Quitin Gunn, Ellen Foster, Rosie Woodfolk, and Wendy Franklin, vocals; Bryant McClinton Fisher, bass/vocals; and Ken Neeley Fisher, bass. This group became just as polished and as successful as any in the program. We had built their self-confidence, their self worth, increased their musical knowledge and goal setting and *"nothing was going to stop them now."*

They performed at many of the events held at the Club as well as functions held within the city. One memorable performance is when they performed with other Boys Club bands at one of the Show Wagons held in the city. See their photo below:

Photo courtesy of Chuck Miller

Classic Quality Band in concert, 1979.

Left to right, back row: Dwayne Tucker, trumpet; Robert Brown, trombone; Ken Neeley Fisher, bass. Left to right, front row: Ellen Foster, vocals, Quincy Gunn, vocals; and Bryant McClinton Fisher, bass/vocals.

156

Photo courtesy of Chuck Miller

Classic Quality Band in concert, 1979.

Left to right, back row: Dwayne Tucker, trumpet; Robert Brown, trombone; Ken Neeley Fisher, bass. Left to right, front row: Ellen Foster, vocals; Quincy Gunn, vocals; and Bryant McClinton Fisher, bass/vocals.

Photo courtesy of Chuck Miller

Quality Band Member, 1979.

Dwayne Tucker, vocals.

Photo courtesy of Chuck Miller

Quality Band Members, 1979.

Bryant McClinton Fisher bass and Michael Tucker, drums.

Photo courtesy of Chuck Miller

Classic Quality Band with all vocalists, 1979.

Left to right, back row: Michael Tucker, drums; Left to right, front row: Rosie Woodfolk, Wendy Franklin, Ellen Foster, & Quincy Gunn, vocals; and Ken Neeley Fisher, bass; Bryant McClinton Fisher, bass/vocals; Dwayne Tucker, trumpet; Robert Brown, trombone; not pictured.

Not only did these students succeed in the programs at the Boys' Club but also they received great success with their attendance and grades at school. This type of success made the Boys' Club program worthwhile. Calvin Howell remembers:

⊔

There were other things going on at the Boy's Club Too. There was a cat that was into Malcolm-X, and since I liked to read, I would at times hang out in the Library and listen to him talk about Black Power or listen to cassette tapes about our rich history of black accomplishment.

I don't remember the bother's name, but he made me proud to be black. In Omaha, we had our experience with the riots after the assassination of Dr. Martin Luther King. Only thing was, I could not understand why my own people were trashing, burning and thrashing OUR OWN neighborhood? If there was to be some burning, I thought they should have been burning somewhere else.

I still remember some of my friends' parents who ran small businesses on 24th Street putting signs in their storefront windows that read "Black Owned". For some of them, it did not help. Actually, Malcolm-X was born just a few blocks from our house on Evans. I think his mother's place was over on Bristol. So, you see, we as young boys at the Boy's Club were getting exposed to many ideas and things that we would have otherwise never encountered." Howell, Calvin, Telephone Interview with Chuck Miller, (11 Jan. 09), Orlando, Florida[xxiv].

⅃

In addition to learning new information about our rich Black Political History, I taught the students new information about our rich Music History, Black Composers, and their application of music theory and performance. I assigned each student the task of listening to and performing recordings of vocalist/instrumentalist, James Brown and American musician/poet Gil Scott-Heron. Their songs were used to increase the self-esteem and self-discipline skills of each musician.

Brown songs made them feel good about them selves and made them become more responsible for the choices they made. A couple of the songs we used are listed below:

1. *"I'm Black and I'm Proud."* This song encouraged the band members to become proud of their race and their heritage; it also became a statement about an emerging sense of black power in 1968.

2. *"This is a Man's World."* This song taught the members the importance of treating women with respect. One of the phrases read: "This is a Man's world, but it would be nothing without a woman or a girl."

Songs about the drug "Heron" made the musicians think twice about starting or continuing using drugs of any kind. A couple of the songs we used are listed below:

3. *"King Heroin."* We used this song as the theme song for our Drug Education Concert. Instead of having a regular music concert, we had the musicians portray the lives of musicians who have died as the results of heroin and other drug usage. A couple of names, which come to mind, are, Janis Joplin and Jimmy Hendrix.

4. *"Angel Dust."* Gil Scott-Heron wrote this song, which by the way was very helpful in getting our point across. Here are words from the chorus of the song: "Angel Dust/Please children would you listen. Angel Dust/Just ain't where it's at. Angel Dust/You won't remember what you're missin', but down some dead end streets there ain't no turnin' back." Angel Dust was a very dangerous drug that destroyed many lives during the late 1970's.

So many of our young people were experimenting with drugs until on February 28, 1980 we decided to sponsor our first "Drug Education Concert," in title, *"Lets Talk About Drugs."* At this concert we had a panel made up of members from various bands that portrayed persons who had a bad experience using drugs. Any member from within the Club was invited to attend.

Photo courtesy of Chuck Miller

Band students reviewing photos for Drug Concert.

Left to right: Matthew Rupert, Thomas Wells, Stanley Tribble & an unidentified student.

The Master of Ceremonies was Gary Williams who introduced the program for the evening. Gary announced that the guide who accompanied the Drug Program list five questions which formed the core of the program: They were as follows: 1.What is a drug? 2. Why are drugs different from anything taken into the body? 3. What kinds of drugs are there? 4. Why do people take drugs? 5. What do drugs do?

The panelists for the event were as follows: Bridgett Johnson as vocalist Janis Joplin, and the late Damien Turner as Jimmy Hendrix. Students then talked about the different types of drugs. Sharon Tucker talked about Aspirins and other drugs in the medicine cabinet. Michael Wair talked about Amphetamines or pep pills. Clarence Majors talked about Barbiturates, (the opposite of Amphetamines). Adolph Williams talked about Marijuana which is the same as Loco Weed. This popular drug is known by many other names. Robin Jones spoke about Cocaine. Charlie Williams spoke about Psychedelic drugs. Karmen Booker presented a summary of all of the panelists.

The Anti Drug Band

Next there was a selection from **the Anti Drug Band** called "Angel Dust." Members of the band were: vocalists Tony Carter, Bridgett Johnson, Gary Williams, Sharon Tucker, Clarence Majors, Michael Wair, piano, the late Damien Turner, guitar, Bryant McClinton Fisher, bass, Adolph Williams, trumpet, Charlie Williams, alto saxophone and Michael Tucker, drums.

The band next performed a selection by vocal James Brown called "King Heroin." This group featured Adolph Williams, vocals, Charlie Williams on alto saxophone, Michael Wair, piano, Bryant McClinton Fisher, bass and Michael Tucker, drums.

There were questions from the audience, which gave personal insights on the use of drugs in our community. This annual event proved to be educational and enlightening.

The Look Band

This next group was one of the best looking groups we had. Bassist Bryant McClinton Fisher remembers how the next group called **"THE LOOK"** got its start:

⌐

Chuck taught us quite a lot about music techniques. So we took everything he taught us and applied it to the music scene. As time pasted I was blessed to be apart of a band which spirit will never be replaced, the name of the band was called The LOOK. The band members were: Ken Brown, drums, Damien Turner, guitar, Mario Branch Corbino lead vocalist, Angie Stennis, keyboards, Carline King, keyboards & vocals, Shawn Washington Lead & Background vocals, & I played the bass.

Thanks to the North Omaha Boy's Club for being a tool used by the oversight of Jehovah GOD & his son Christ Jesus, I can say our lives were blessed for having a teacher, a father figure, and a friend who cared for us as, Mr. Miller. Fisher McClinton, Bryant, Telephone Interview with Chuck Miller, (11 Jan. 09), Nebraska, Omaha.[xxv]

⌐

The group is pictured below:

Photo courtesy of Bryant McClinton Fisher

The LOOK Band, 1980.

Left to right back row: The late Damien Turner, guitar; Bryant McClinton Fisher, bass; Left to right middle row: Carline King, keyboards & vocals; Shawn Washington Lead & Background vocals; Angie Stennis, keyboards, kneeling; Ken Brown, drums; and not pictured, Mario Branch Corbino, lead vocalist.

Photo courtesy of Bryant McClinton Fisher

The LOOK Band member & Leader, 1980.

Bryant McClinton Fisher, bass.

The LOOK was a very polished group with a fresh look on the scene. With their colorful outfits and professional look, they were a crown pleaser every time they performed. Soon they were in demand and they performed all over Omaha and frequently perform some out of town engagements.

Funktion Band

A few of the members of the Look Band later organized a new group called **Funktion**; they are shown in the photo below.

Photo courtesy of Bryant McClinton Fisher

Funktion Band at Rehearsal, 1980.

Left to right back row: Stevie Houston, keyboard player; Ken Brown, drums; Bryant McClinton Fisher, bass; the late Damien Turner, guitar; Left to right front row: Mario Branch Corbino lead vocalist; and Quincy Gunn, vocals.

Jam Inc. Band

This next group was called **"JAM INC."** Their ages ranged from eight to twelve. This group opened a concert for the nationally known group **"SWITCH"** and was offered a chance to be managed by Michael Jackson's brother, Jermaine of the famous group *The Jackson 5*.

Jermaine was very impressed with the attitude and talent of these young people and wanted to give them a chance at success at an early age. However, the parents of the group thought they were too young to leave school and wanted the group to wait until they were a little older before committing themselves.

Jermaine's offer was a great honor for the band and it helped add inspiration and shined a light and a ray of hope in these precious young lives, an honor they will never forget. The group is pictured below:

Photo courtesy of Chuck Miller

Jam Inc. Band in Concert, 1981.

Left to right back row: Clarence Nichols, guitar; Robert Smith, drums; Stanley Robinson, bass. Left to right front row: Craig Nelson, trumpet, kneeling; Kirk Devine, percussion; and Mario Branch Corbino, lead vocalist.

The secret to their success was centered on my ability to re-arrange the music to fit the musician and the band as a whole. This ability to re-arrange the music was inspired by noticing how my mother, the late Mrs. Essie Ree Futch Miller dresses. She was a young beautiful lady and a great dresser.

Everything she wore looked great on her. She knew how to choose the right earrings to match her face and her clothes. The furs she wore seem to blend right in with her skin color. Her hats were always centered on her head even if they were worn to the left or right, they always seem to complement her overall dress style. Notice these ideas in her photo below:

Photo courtesy of Chuck Miller

My mother.
The Late Mrs. Essie Ree Futch Miller in her early 20's.

I took these ideas and used them whenever I wrote music for any of the bands. Whenever one of the younger musicians was faced with an advanced chord voicing to play, I would use a hybrid structure to create the voicing. One of the chord sounds used in many of the songs was the $G^{13\,sus\,4}$ chord.

I simply had the young guitarist or pianist play an F Maj ^{7} chord while the bass player played a G note. The $G^{13\,sus\,4}$ chord symbols would end up looking like this: F Maj 7/G. This idea worked great and made a complicated chord progression seem easy to play for the musicians.

When arranging music for horn players, I again looked to my mother for inspiration. As my mother would look deep inside of her mind to choose the right apparel to compliment her dress, I did the same. I learned to take a recording of a song and look deep inside the arrangement to find the parts I wanted the musicians to play. I would choose notes that would not normally be heard by most ears and use them to develop my arrangements. This technique worked great and it confused many of my competitors for decades.

Destiny Band

The only all female group to form in Omaha was called "**Destiny**." They were great friends of the Boys Club band members. Everywhere the Boys Club bands performed, Destiny was not to far away. This was a very good group who could really play and perform quite well. The group is pictured below:

Photo courtesy of Shonda Grayer Johnson

Destiny, The early years.

From left to right: row one: Crystal Gresham, vocals; Alesia Lynch, vocals; Melony Watkins, vocals; from left to right: row two, Shonda Grayer Johnson, keyboards/background vocals; Edna McAlister, lead/rhythm guitar; Ginger "Dee" Davis, drums; Lisa McIntosh, (not pictured), bass guitar.

Photo courtesy of Shonda Grayer Johnson

Destiny, The Classic Group.

From left to right: row one, Ginger "Dee" Davis, drums; Edna McAllister, lead/rhythm guitar; The late Carol Bullion Terrell, keyboards and vocals; from left to right: row two, Melony Watkins, vocals; Bridgette Jones, vocals; Crystal Gresham, vocals; from left to right: row three, Shonda Grayer Johnson, keyboards/vocals, and Alesia Lynch, vocals.

This popular group was inducted into the Omaha Black Music Hall of Fame in the summer of 2007. A complete biography of the group was listed on the Hall of Fame web site. I thought it would be great to list it here in its entirety:

Ⅱ

2007 Inductee, Destiny:

Destiny was founded in the summer of 1983, with the following members: Shonda Grayer Johnson, Alesia Lynch,

Crystal Gresham, and Bridgette Jones. These four ladies became well-known around Omaha for their dynamic voices and their unforgettable harmonizing style as well as their impeccable beauty.

After long hard and tiresome basement practices, they decided it was time to take Omaha by storm. Their first performance was a talent show sponsored by the North Omaha Boys Club under the direction of Mr. Chuck Miller. With the help of Mr. James Boone, Destiny was featured in Omaha's own Go-A-Head Magazine.

Destiny now decided it was time to elevate to higher heights, by adding musicians to the unit. After a long hard search, Destiny finally found the core of what would become Omaha's "All Female Band." Added musicians were Carol Bullion, keyboardist; Edna McAllister, lead/rhythm guitar; Lisa McIntosh, bass guitar; and Ginger "Dee" Davis, drummer. Now Destiny was ready to hit the scene in Omaha, this unit was complete.

They appeared at all of the popular spots in Omaha and surrounding areas: NCO Club at the Offutt Air force Base, Bellevue; Nuncios; Just Us; The Backstreet Lounge, Cateekas; The Grapevine Lounge; The Ranch Bowl; Club 89; Dreamers; and The Nebraska State Penitentiary in Lincoln.

Destiny began to do bigger and better things including traveling, writing/performing their own original tunes. With the talent of each member they wrote and arranged memorable songs such as "Time will tell" & "Baby I'm Hooked"...and the song that made you "Get up off of that Stuff."

Then came the time when Destiny had to make an intensifying decision. Lisa Mac, the bassist, enlisted in the Armed Forces and had to be replaced. What was once one of the only all female bands around, the unit would now have to add a male. With no funky female bass players around the area in the 80', Lisa Mac's replacement was the legendary Charles "OilCan" Jones, already very well known and respected on the scene; he became a big brother to all the ladies in the group.

With this unit and the addition of power vocalists, Melony Watkins, Destiny traveled and performed in Dallas, Texas; South/North Dakota, Des Moines, Iowa; Kansas City, MO; and surrounding areas; and were chosen to be the opening act for world-renowned national recording artist, MidNight Starr.

Destiny continued on into the early 90's musically through the ebb and flow; the ups, downs and disappointments of the Omaha music scene. Members were also developing other musical interests. Constantly having to prove themselves as viable musicians and artists; the desire to start families; the inevitable growth of talent in this unit; along with the constant personnel changes, lead to the disbanding of this talented Omaha first.

The members of Destiny formed a special bond that will always exist in our hearts, the fans that we touched; our extended family of fellow musicians and our families. Our Hearts are full of everlasting love as we remember our special sister Carol Bullion Terrell. Rest in peace. The Omaha Black Music Hall of Fame, summer of 2007.[xxvi]

⅃

The group's drummer said it best when she identified the character of each musician, she writes:

ᘛ

Shonda-the "shy" one busting with energy, these huge amazing vocals and subtle sex appeal; Patti, Twinkie, "Retha and them.

Bridgette-the "humming bird" sweet buttery sensual vocals, hip swaying crooner and folks crying; Minnie, Whitney and Denise-throw in a little Dinah.

Crystal-the "harmonizer" and perfectionist;" go to"-the one who had confidence when none of us had any, ultra smooth. One of the only ones actively employed.......Gladys, Tremaine, Mavis.

Edna-our "secret weapon", the fire, the quiet storm; straight NO-Chaser, singin, cussin, playin and prayin in all at the same time! The only one who could "read" for real... Bunny, Prince, CeCe.

Alesia-the "passion fruit," our nucleus-our very energy depended on her, she could pull a bad day together and we'd have the most amazing gig ever-the life-blood; can sing, dance and make you believe again.......Regina, Lena, Chaka, Janet.

Melony-the "phenomenon" breathing new life into us when we were disenchanted, the breeze, the Amazon, the belter, the machine, the go-getter....... Tina, Jennifer, LaBelle.

Charles-the "groove,", taught us how to add the mature touch to the music, laid-back teacher, showed us we were just as good as the guys, made us want to be better musicians..............BabyFace in demeanor, LA in playing, Stanley, Marcus.

Ginger-the "cohesion," tried hard to keep us together, the one to talk to; made the guys pay attention; demanded people to respect us, the director, lady emcee-Cindy, Angela, Latifah.

Carol-our "big sister," did the best she could with us all, tried to keep us encouraged added the "show" aspect to the group. "Made" us write original music when we wanted to be somebody else.....Patti Austin, Patrice, Bayer-Sager. Ginger "Dee" Davis, Destiny's drummer.[xxvii]

⅃

This group truly had it all: poise, beauty, style, grace, talent and much more. They were indeed tops in their field. You were pretty great also, OilCan!

Destine became great friends with many of the Boys Club students bands. They also became good friends with bands I organized of my own. My groups were organized using students and adults from the community.

Chuck Miller & The Persuaders Band

The first group was called, "***Chuck Miller & The Persuaders***" which featured John Butler and Sam Singleton, vocalists; Eric Johnson, bass; Keith Nelson, guitar; Earl Page, organ; and Eddie Gaines percussionist. The group is pictured below:

Dancing With A "Soul Band"

CHUCK MILLER & THE PERSUADERS

Members of Chuck Miller & The Persuaders: From left to right (front row) are John Butler, Chuck Miller, Sam Singleton, and Eric Johnson. From left to right (back row) are Earl Page, Keith Nelson and Eddie Gaines.

"Dancing In The Dark"   **"Unforgettable"**

Fairbury Junior College lads and lasses had an enjoyable evening this month while dancing by the delicate "SOUL MUSIC" of CHUCK MILLER & THE PERSUADERS. The event was the annual Homecoming Ball at which the Miller ensemble was invited to perform.

Photo courtesy of Chuck Miller

This Year's Replacement Band

Chuck Miller & The Persuaders eventually became "***This Year's Replacement***," which featured the late Lonzo Franklin, vocalist; Steven Smith, trumpet; Tony, guitar; Paul Jelkins, trumpet; Garie Crowder, bass; Leonard Harris, organ; Timmy Winfrow, and Jim Jelkins, percussionist; and Chuck Miller, tenor saxophone/leader.

Photo courtesy of Chuck Miller

This Years Replacement Band Horn Section.

From left to right: Row one, Paul Jelkins, trumpet; Steven Smith, trumpet; Chuck Miller, tenor saxophone/vocals.

Photo courtesy of Chuck Miller

This Years Replacement Band.

From left to right: row one, the late Lonzo Franklin, lead vocals; Steven Smith, trumpet; Chuck Miller, tenor saxophone/vocals.

Poverty's Movement Band

This Year's Replacement eventually became "**Poverty's Movement**," which featured Roosevelt Collins organ, Garie Crowder bass, Hank Thomas tenor saxophone, Lois Eleby (a.k.a. Lady Mac) guitar, J0hnny Butler vocals; Vernon Martin soon replaced Johnny Butler as vocalist, Larry Smith percussionist and Chuck Miller, trumpet/vocals/leader.

The group name was changed to better relate the type of notes they stroke. Poverty Movement soon recorded a 45 RPM entitled "Heartbreak" which became a hit in the community. The group featured an attractive young lady, Lois Eleby who was rated with the best guitarist in the Midwest. Producer Jim Calloway wrote an interesting comment about the group in his October, 1971 issue of Black Scene Magazine:

LL

Jim Calloway, Poverty's Movement Will Move You:

I'm sure that many of you will agree with me when I say that "it's hard to find a good band with a good sound that can hold the attention of an audience in Omaha." Well, believe it or not, after a good 5 years of listening to ordinary, so called rock groups, I've found out that Omaha has been blessed with a band with a taste of talent. Poverty's Movement (previously known as The Persuaders) has come a long way in the last year and from the sounds of things, they'll be going a lot further in the future.

The group, composed of 5 male members and one female, is what I consider to be the best all around band in the state – or Midwest as far as that's concerned. Not only can they make your feet pat to the sound of soul but they are one of the few groups that insert choreography into their routine to add icing to the cake.

Many of you probably remember the Smokers of 1965 – 1968 fame who have always been considered the most versatile group ever to emerge from the city. Well, I don't think that I could compare Poverty's Movement with them but I would go so far as to say that they would rank a second.

The whole group is weaved together as tight as my billfold (and that's tight) and in my opinion there is one member who really stands out. Not that I'm partial to saxophone players but the group's sax man rates an extra star for his performance on tunes like Misty and Harlem Nocturne. When it comes to solos it seems like he slides through them like a hot iron on ice.

To break it down, he's one of the soul-full sax men within a 200 – mile radius of the city. At present, the group is performing at Gino's Lounge at 717 S. 16th St. According to new club owner Nelson Griffey, the group will be there indefinitely and you can't blame him. If you're the type that likes and appreciates soulful music and a professional show, take my advice and check this group out. Be sure to get there before 10:00 p.m., otherwise you'll be greeted with "standing room only." Calloway, Jim, (Black Scene Magazine), October, 1971, Omaha, Nebraska.[xxviii]

The group is pictured below:

Photo courtesy of Chuck Miller

Poverty Movement.

From left to right: Row one, Garie L. Crowder, bass; Chuck Miller, trumpet/vocals; Lois Eleby, guitar; from left to right: row two, Henry "Hank" Thomas, tenor saxophone/vocals; Larry Smith, drums; Roosevelt Collins, organ; and Vernon Martin, lead vocals.

Chazz Band

Poverty Movement eventually became "***Chazz***," which featured Sam Singleton vocalist; Lois Eleby McMorris (a.k.a. Lady Mac) guitar; Leonard Harris organ; Bobby Griffo tenor saxophone; Ray, percussionist; and Chuck Miller, trumpet/vocalist/leader.

Photo courtesy of Chuck Miller

Chazz Band, 1975-76.

From left to right: Row one, Ray, percussion; Chuck Miller, trumpet/vocals/leader; Garie Crowder, bass; from left to right: row two, Bobby Griffo, tenor saxophone; Sam Singleton, lead vocals; Leonard Harris, organ; Lois McMorris, guitar; unidentified conga player.

There were many bands playing in the city at this time. Chazz went through some personnel changes. Drummer, Hank Davis, replaced Ray as percussionist. See comments below in The Air Pulse News Paper.

⌐

The group "Chazz" entertained at the Recreation Center at Offutt Air Force Base on Sunday from 9 p.m. until midnight. The NCO club will cater. The Air Pulse, January 22, 1975.[xxix]

⌐

See the new group Chazz in the photo below.

Photo courtesy of Chuck Miller

Omaha Rock/Jazz Group "Chazz", 1976.

From left to right: Row one, Garie Crowder, bass; Lois McMorris, guitar; Chuck Miller, trumpet/vocals/leader; from left to right: row two, Bobby Griffo, tenor saxophone; Hank Davis, drums; Leonard Harris, organ. Sam Singleton, lead vocals; not pictured.

Master Chazz Band

Chazz became ***Master Chazz***, which featured Doug Holstrum piano; and Sam Singleton, vocals, not pictured;

Thomas Wells bass; Hank Thomas tenor saxophone; Gary Williams, percussion; and Chuck Miller, trumpet/vocalist. Clarence Nichols was later added on guitar; Stanley Tribble replaced Thomas Wells on bass. There is no photo of this group. The group later experienced some more personnel changes which made it a larger group. This larger group is pictured below:

Photo courtesy of Chuck Miller

Master Chazz Band.

From left to right: Row one, Chuck Miller, trumpet/vocals/leader; Carmen Booker, lead vocals; Thomas Wells, bass; Paula Lollar, lead vocals; Henry "Hank" Thomas, tenor saxophone; from left to right: row two, Gary Williams, drums; Earl Page, organ.

This larger group soon experienced some personnel changes and younger members from the Boys Club were brought into the group. More hope was brought into the lives of these young musicians when something spectacular happened during a television show shooting called "Black on Black" with host, the great late legendary jazz alto saxophonist, Preston Love.

The group Master Chazz, named after me, was performing our version of the hit song, "Ain't No Stopping Us Now." The band consisted of five members: Henry "Hank" Thomas played tenor saxophone and sung background vocals, Clarence Nichols (twelve years old at the time) played guitar; Stanley Tribble (thirteen years old at the time) played bass; and Gary Williams (seventeen years old at the time) played drums and sung lead and background vocals; and I played keyboards, trumpet and sung lead and background vocals.

The thing that made this shooting so special and put the band's name among those who were first in doing something that had never been done by a local band before, was *when we formed a front line and did a dance routine during the break of the song*.

This was a routine I often saw groups like the Temptations and the Four Tops do. The only exception was, the Temptations and Four Tops' groups were specifically designed for the purpose of doing dance routines during their performances and the Master Chazz band was not.

However, Master Chazz managed to assimilate this routine by having Gary Williams come off of the drums, I came from behind the keyboards and join Henry "Hank" Thomas and form the front line. While the guitar and bass continued to play a rhythmic accompaniment, *the three musicians performed a short dance routine that could be equaled to any.* This concept was new to local musicians in the Omaha area. See their photo below:

Photo courtesy of Chuck Miller

Original Master Chazz Band, Black on Black T.V. Show, 1980.

From left to right: Row one, Clarence Nichols, guitar; Chuck Miller, trumpet/vocals/leader; Henry "Hank" Thomas, tenor saxophone; from left to right: row two, Gary Williams, drums; Stanley Tribble, bass guitar.

The Master Chazz Band of 1981 featured Clifford Moore, vocals; Gary Williams, drums; Bryant McClinton Fisher, bass; Doug Holstrom, keyboards; Jesse Wallace, guitar; and Chuck Miller, keyboards/ trumpet/ vocals.

There were still some more personnel changes made. Richard Thomas replaced Gary Williams on drums; Thomas Wells returned to bass, Eddie Grant replaced Richard Thomas on drums; and Mario Branch Corbino was added as vocalist. The group is pictured below:

Master Chazz Band.

From left to right: Row one, Eddie Grant, drums; Chuck Miller, trumpet/vocal/keyboards/leader; Doug Holstrom, keyboards; from left to right: row two, Mario Corbino, lead vocals; Jesse Wallace, guitar; and Thomas Wells, bass.

This group became very popular and got many chances to open for some professional groups. They once open a concert at Peony Park for The Dazz Band. What a night that was. First, we went to their sound check and stage preparation. It was great meeting the band, watching them rehearse and finally getting the opportunity to perform on stage using their sound equipment. Their performance was outstanding and we didn't do to bad either. In fact, the group and the crowd loved us also.

Eddie Grant wrote an interesting story about the group and the battle of the bands at the Clouds Night club in Omaha, which opened the door to our performance with The Dazz Band. See his comments below:

⅃

We entered a <u>Battle of The Bands Contest</u> at a Club called The Clouds. ETC, Jam Squad, Nate Bray's Band and some others were contestants also. They were trying to determine who was going to open up for The Dazz Band at Peony Park. We won this event. We had some great equipment and Gary Crowder did a great mix. We didn't even play that long and the people said: You guys are hot!

Members of the group were: Thomas Wells, bass, Doug Holstroms, keyboards, Chuck Miller, keyboards, trumpet and vocals, Jesse Wallace, guitar, Mario Corbino, vocals, Carmon Baylor, vocals and Eddie Grant, drums.

ETC band wouldn't get on stage after they heard us perform. When we finished playing, the people came up to the stage and tried to pull our clothes off, they treated us like stars, and we were cooking! The other bands were up set with us. We were so polished until we didn't have to play that many songs, the audience started clapping before we stopped playing. What a night that was!

Our rehearsals were very well organized, therefore; everything worked out right when it was time to perform. We use to form a circle before we performed and we would say a little prayer to aid us in our performance. So religion played a great part in our success. We performed in a Star Search Concert in west Omaha, but they cheated us. The Judge took off and went to Chicago. He tried to get the Ventriloquist act to be the winner, but we were the real winners. Our vocalist, Sam Rogers just cried and cried; he was so up-set. Grant, Eddie, (Battle of the bands at the Clouds), Telephone Interview with Chuck Miller, (13 Jan. 09), Omaha, Nebraska.[xxx]

The group experienced some more personnel changes and Bobby Hilliard was added as vocalist and Matthew Rupert replaced Eddie Grant as percussionist. In all, there were three versions of the Master Chazz Band. The Classic Master Chazz Band is pictured below:

Photo Courtesy of Chuck Miller

The Classic Master Chazz Band.

From left to right: Row one, Thomas Wells, bass; Chuck Miller, trumpet/keyboards/vocals/leader; Mario Corbino, lead vocals; from left to right: row two, Bobby Hilliard, lead vocals; Matthew Rupert, drums; Jesse Wallace, guitar.

Square Biz Band

The Master Chazz Band eventually became "**Square Biz**," which featured David Bailey, bass; Everett (EJ) Jackson replaced David Bailey on bass and background vocals; Jesse Wallace, guitar, Mario Branch Corbino, Paula Lollar, Sharon Watson and Daryl Jackson vocalists; Matthew Rupert and Chris Poulton, percussionist; and Chuck Miller trumpet/vocals. There was an interesting article published in the Omaha Star News Paper, see the article below:

⊩

*On July 31, 1986, the headlines from the Omaha Star News paper read: **"Square Biz" Takes Omaha By Storm**. It went on to say: after months of rehearsing, "Square Biz" can be proud of themselves. They've performed for weddings, jammed at music sessions with top local musicians, appeared on a show packed with two of the leading groups in Omaha and scored very high in a local talent show. But what was "Square Biz" really like? According to group leader Chuck Miller, "this is not a band, this is a passionate case of possession, more than that – it's the biggest gamble happening in local modern soul/top 40. If these young people could get it together fully, magnifying all their strengths and canceling out all their weaknesses, they could crack the whole music industry like a whip."*

After listening to this dynamic group, it is fairly easy to tell that the group is well rehearsed and polished. Since 90% of their music is first arranged and scored on manuscript modern technology plays an important part – multi-track recorders and video cassette tape recorders are used to monitor most of their rehearsals, it allows the seven piece group to alter any portion of their performance at will.

Its classic group was formed when everyone was replaced except the percussionist, Matthew Rupert. Square Biz was a funk/jazz music band that enjoyed enormous popularity in Omaha, Nebraska and the surrounding states in the mid 1980s. The name of the band was conceived when leader Chuck Miller heard a recording by vocalist Teena Marie called *Square Biz*. Among their biggest cover hits were the songs *"Slow Jam"* by Midnight Star, *"Careless Whispers"* by Wham, *"Knock Knock"* by Dazz, *"Thriller"* by Michael Jackson, *"Wichita Lineman"* (the jazz version), by Glen Campbell and *"Purple Rain"* by Prince.

The group is pictured below:

Photo courtesy of Chuck Miller

Square Biz, The Classic Group.

From left to right: Row one, Charles "Oil Can" Jones, bass; Denise Taylor, lead vocals; Robert Holmes, lead and rhythm guitar; Standing, left to right: row two, Chuck Miller, trumpet, keyboards and vocals; Matthew Rupert, percussion; Charles "Chucky" Robinson, keyboards; Samuel Rogers, lead vocals.

CHUCK MILLER, *standing back row left to right, #1, keyboard synthesis/lead and back- up vocals and manager has many talents in many areas. His national professional experience includes: recording and performing with The Esquires & The Fabulous Rhinestones and The Paul Butterfield Blues Band. He has also appeared in concert with Loggins and Messina, The Dazz*

Band, Switch, New Edition, jazz guitarist Kenny Burrell and Grover Washington, Jr. Chuck is a graduate of the University of Nebraska at Omaha, a graduate of The University of Nebraska in Lincoln, Nebraska and a graduate of Rutgers University's Mason Gross School of the Arts in New Brunswick, New Jersey. He also attended Berklee College of Music in Boston, Mass for a year. He is currently a Professor of Music for Music In Catholic Schools Bands and a former Adjunct Professor for the Black Studies Department at the University of Nebraska at Omaha.

MATTHEW RUPERT, standing back row left to right, #2, Drummer/percussionist, has often said, "music is my life." His bouncing beat is the pacesetter for the group. As drummer, his timing is precise. Matthew's musical tastes are varied: they include soul, jazz, pop, classical and rock. The replacements were as follows:

CHARLES L. ROBINSON, standing back row left to right, #3, keyboard synthesis/back-up vocals. He gained considerable experience playing in many now defunct groups such as Electrified Soul, L.C. and The Outsiders Blues Band. Last Chance and Cream of the Crop. His keyboard style is a unique duplication of his vocal style – linear and melodic. Chuck is also a fine percussionist. He performs on congas, kalimba and the drum set.

SAMUEL D. ROGERS, standing back row left to right, #4, lead vocalist/keyboard & drums, got his start in the church. He has grown into an all-around performer who loves to communicate a message through his songs. His moves are dynamic. His voice quality is just as good as Stevie Wonder, Ray Charles or any one else in the professional vocal music industry. Sam also serves as the group's choreographer.

CHARLES R.A. JONES III, sitting front row left to right, #1, bassist/back-up vocals. His stage name is "Oil Can," a name given to him by legendary musicians of the Omaha area. Charles has performed and recorded in Los Angeles with such groups as Martha Reeves, The Drifters, N.Y. L.A. Band, Puzzle People Band and Steinbeck Pro. He is the nephew of nationally known jazz singer Sarah Vaughn and is also related to Wilson Picket.

***DENISE TAYLOR**, sitting front row left to right, #2, lead vocals/keyboard synthesis/costume seamstress, is the centerpiece of the group. Not only does she thrill audiences with her charm and good looks but also is a definite asset to the group. One can always move and groove with her while she sings the up-tempo songs, "Get Into the Groove" and "Dress You Up" by Madonna. On the other hand, one can relax and reminisce while she sings the slow songs, "Through The Fire" by Chaka Khan and "Slow Jam" by Midnight Star. She gives credit to Chaka Khan and Midnight Star as being direct influences. "My favorite entertainers range from Flora Purim, to Luciano Pavarotti, to Chaka Khan. I love it all." Nesi use to dream of becoming an entertainer. After studying piano for 13 years and attending Drake University on music scholarship, her dream has now come true.*

***ROBERT HOLMES**, sitting front row left to right, #3, guitarist, was born and raised in Philadelphia and began playing the guitar at the age of 12. He feels very lucky to have been raised around the Philadelphia international influence. He has been associated with the Delphonics and the Intruders, but was most influenced by the late Jimi Hendrix.*

As you can see, this was one of the hottest groups during its time. They performed at many of the prestigious nightclubs in Omaha and surrounding states. Their last performance was in Omaha at the 20's Lounge where they were asked to perform for a birthday party for the wife of the great owner of the 20's, Mickie's. The Omaha Star, "Square Biz" Takes Omaha By Storm, Omaha, Nebraska, July 31, 1986.[xxxi]

Square Biz Band has produced musicians who have gone on to becoming great professionals in their own rights. Many of them are still performing and producing recordings for others. The group recorded one album on the Selah Sound Record Label with many of the hits of the day. Their influence and musical style lives on in many of the local bands today.

One of the better known groups that became equally popular in the performance arena as any one in Omaha was the Steppen Stonz. Along with most of the groups mentioned in this book, they were inducted into the Black Music Hall of Fame. Andre Stennis, one of the Boys Club's most popular drummers was their drummer. Andre also performed in the following Boys Club groups: Master Chazz, Chazz, Jam Squad and Square Biz. The group sent me an interesting card from London during their European overseas tour. See the card below:

Photo courtesy of Chuck Miller

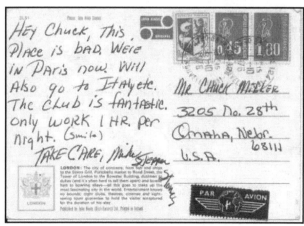

Photo courtesy of Chuck Miller

Card from the Steppen Stonz, European Overseas Tour.

An interesting biography of the group appeared on the Internet, it is mentioned below in its entirety:

⌐

In 1972, then called "The Magnificent Men", they began with a modest one-night gig during Black Heritage week in Omaha, Nebraska. The group was later joined by four very talented musicians who also resided in the Omaha area. Glenn Franklin (drummer), Keith Rogers (keyboards), Melvin Hall (bassist) and Ernie Clark (lead guitar). These young gentlemen were the original backbone and the driving force of the Magnificent Men show. With the three vocalists it was said together they made music magic. Soon they were performing at night clubs and concerts, opening for recording artist such as Blood Stone, Kool and the Gang and the Chi-Lites. They were also featured on a local Omaha television show for two years that made them local celebrities. After leaving Omaha in 1974, their musical career led them on a cross country tour. The group spent several weeks touring through the states of Iowa, Missouri, Oklahoma, Arizona and ending in San Diego, California.

After performing and residing in San Diego for a short while, they finally worked their way into the Los Angeles area in 1974. There, they performed in night clubs and was fortunate enough to be able to experience recording in some of Los Angeles finest recording studios of the time. Their name was then changed from The Magnificent Men to The Steppen Stones for recording purposes. This new name reflected the groups high energy and intricate dance steps. During this time, the group was approached by two producers from A&M Records. Two songs were then written for the group. "You Can't Squeeze Blood From A Stone" and "Dancin Power". Neither song was released. Even though they didn't produce a hit record, The Steppen Stones were determined not to let that stifle their musical career. They resided in the Los Angeles area until the local night clubs had totally switched from live bands to DJ's and disco dance clubs. While disco was quickly spreading throughout Southern California in the late seventies, The Pacific Northwest was very much alive with live entertainment night clubs and hotels from Portland, Oregon to Vancouver, Canada. In 1977, the group was booked into Portland, Oregon and there they performed several weeks, touring the local night clubs. After fulfilling contractual obligations in Portland, The Steppen Stones musicians decided to disband and pursue other musical career opportunities. The following year the three vocalists re-grouped and they were again invited to perform in The Pacific Northwest. Only this time, the group was booked into the Seattle, Washington night club scene and shortly thereafter, Seattle became their new home base. This kept The Steppen Stones career alive and on track.

Now settled into Seattle, the group decided they wanted to return back into the recording studio. Their close friend and manager the late Joe Nozzarella suggested releasing a record under their own lable, named J.A.M. (John, Arthur, Mike) records. Joe was very involved in the production of the recording sessions. There was a single released in 1979 entitled "COME TO ME". The record received some airplay on one of Seattle's popular radio stations and was distributed to some of Tacoma and Seattle, Washington's local record stores. The record sales were up and they made the Top Ten best seller list. That same year, another song on the flip side of the featured single entitled "DARLIN OH DARLIN" was featured on the long running television show American Bandstand "Rate a Record". The record was rated a 77% which was high enough to beat out the veteran recording artist Fats Domino's new single. This was said to be a very high rating for a nationally unknown group. Both songs were written by two very talented musicians from Tacoma. Regrettably, there were legal battles over the rights of the songs and the project was canceled. Soon thereafter, The Steppen Stones dropped the songs from their live show performances. Another recording opportunity came their way during 1985. The group was again invited to Los Angeles to record backup vocals for another recording artist which was being produced by Ralph Johnson, an original member of the famed group EARTH, WIND AND FIRE and co-produced by Marcel East, another well known record producer. Together, they produced a record called HOLD ME TIGHT. After finishing these projects and from the exposure of being in The Pacific Northwest, The Steppen Stones continued their career and soon after expanded into Nevada. Their first booking into the Nevada area was Reno in 1981. In 1990 the spelling of "Stones" was changed to "Stonz" for an updated appeal and the rest is history.

The group now features two male vocalists; Arthur Hayden and Michael Hill (friends since kindergarten) have been performing together for 37 years providing lead vocals, harmonies and choreography, along with fourteen year member Andre Stennis on drums, and vocals, is what makes The Steppen Stonz so much fun to watch and listen to.

In May of 2005 the Steppen Stonz performed in the half time show in Philadelphia for Bon Jovi one of the owners of the Philadelphia Soul Arena Football Team.
http://www.steppenstonz.com/id7.html[xxxii]. They can be seen in the photo below:

Photo http://www.steppenstonz.com/id8.html[xxiii]

The Steppen Stonz with Bon Jobi

From left to right: Michael Hill, the late John Matthews, Bon Jobi, Arthur Hayden and Andre Stennis.

Photo http://www.steppenstonz.com/id4.html[xxiv]

The Steppen Stonz, Black Music Hall Of Fame...2007.

From left to right: Row one: Arthur, and Michael. Row two: Left to right: Bobby, Glenn (original member), Andre, Ernie and Melvin (original members).

Out of all of the bands on the scene, which included: Top Secret, Man Verses Man, New Breed of Soul, Shades & Danger, Brass Rhythm & Funk, Intensity, Leonard Williams' Blues Band, and The Jail Breakers, only Jam Squad and Square Biz were direct competition for this next group called E.T.C.?

E.T.C. band was the epitome of all of the Boys Club bands. Some of its members were in that first group of at-risk youngsters that broke into the pawn shop. They experienced many things that should have eliminated them from the music scene. However, this gave them the edge over the other groups; they were not only a good band but they were over comers. They were determined that nothing was going to stop them from reaching their goal of performing throughout the US and abroad. See their story in the next chapter.

7

E.T.C. BAND

The group Contact merged into a group called "**E.T.C.**," one of the most successful groups to develop from The Club. The initials E.T.C. stands for *Entertainment with a Touch of Class*. They performed nationally and internationally and many of its members are still performing in major U.S. cities and Japan during the writing of this book. Members of the band can be seen in the photo below:

Photo courtesy of Chuck Miller

Classic E.T.C. Band Promotional photo, 1982.

Row one kneeling, left to right: Michael B. Adams 2nd, keyboards;
Adolph Williams, trumpet; Greg Bowie, bass; Row two standing, left to right:
Jerry "Duke" Riggs, drums; Roderick Jones, vocals; Gary Williams, vocals;
and Charlie Williams, tenor saxophone.

Photo courtesy of Chuck Miller

E.T.C. Band, 1982.

Row one sitting, left to right: Gary Williams, vocals; Roderick Jones, vocals; Greg Bowie, bass; Row two sitting, left to right: Michael B. Adams 2nd, keyboards; Jerry "Duke" Riggs, drums; Row three standing: Adolph Williams, trumpet; and Charlie Williams, tenor saxophone not pictured.

E.T.C. band became one of the best bands to hit the local scene. They had it all. They could play, sing, talk/communicate and dance; attributes most bands did not have during their hayday. They were tops in their class. Sibyl Myers wrote an interesting article in the Omaha World Herald, which highlights the group, and its accomplishments. I thought it would be worthy to be listed in its entirety here:

⊔

E.T.C. Adds Touch of Class to Music

Omaha World Herald
May 30, 1982
By Sibyl Myers
World Herald Staff Writer

The E.T.C. band is "really tearing up in North Omaha," according to Chuck Miller, director of the Music/Drama Department at the North Omaha Boys' Club.

"They're more popular than any local black bands I've seen in a long time," Miller said.

E.T.C., which stands for "Entertainment with a Touch of Class," consists of six Omahans who range in age from 19 to 22.

E.T.C is ...standing, from left*: Michael B. Adams, 2ⁿᵈ Adolph Williams, Jerry Riggs and Gregory Bowie; seated, from left, Roderick Jones and Gary Williams.*

Members are: Gary Williams and Roderick Jones, lead vocals; Adolph Williams, trumpet, flugelhorn and background vocals; Gregory Bowie, bass and background vocals; Jerry Riggs, drums and Michael Adams II, keyboards. The group's manager is Adams' father, Michael B. Adams 2nd, and Robbie Glover is technician.

The group plays a variety of music including soul, rhythm and blues, jazz blues, and pop. At a dance earlier this year, they opened the set with a waltz. E.T.C. was organized about seven years ago. The present members have been together about two years.

"Great Potential"

The group has "great potential and a good possibility of making it nationally,"

Music

said Paul Allen of the Showcase Lounge where many nationally known black musicians have performed. Allen has been involved in the music business for 35 years and has promoted a number of acts at the City Auditorium including James Brown, Jackie Wilson, Sam Cooke and Dionne Warwick. Drummer Buddy Miles got his start at the Showcase and later wrote a song entitled, "Paul B. Allen, Omaha, Nebraska."

Allen said he recently was in Las Vegas where he saw groups that are not as good as E.T.C. "They read music well; they're well trained and well-disciplined. Their showmanship is excellent."

E.T.C. performs tunes popularized by other musicians such as George Benson, The Jackson's, and Kool and the Gang. This month, Sound Recorders Studios in Omaha will release a record with two originals songs by the group.

"Time on you"

Michael B. Adams 2nd wrote the music and lyrics for a ballad entitled "Time on You." Gary Williams wrote the music and lyrics to "Hummin'," an upbeat tune about actions speaking louder than words. E.T.C. averages about four performances a week. Many engagements are dances sponsored by local black social and civic groups. They also have performed regularly at the Showcase and Back Street Lounges in North Omaha and have appeared at Howard Street Tavern in the Old Market.

Last year, E.T.C. provided the music for Mayor Boyle's Inauguration, and the group was the opening act for the Curtis Blow and Instant Funk concert at the Auditorium. In addition to trips to Lincoln and Sioux City, upcoming engagements will include appearances in Albuquerque, Topeka and Wichita. Locally, Connie Brice is organizing a fan club.

Boys Club Start

Music careers of E.T.C. members have been balanced with part time jobs and school. In addition, the group is renovating an old bus for travel purposes. The bus will be carpeted and have seven beds. Other work has included putting in electricity and making storage compartments for musical equipment.

E.T.C. got its start at the Gene Eppley North Omaha Boys Club through a music program begun by Chuck Miller in 1975 to teach at-risk youth music theory and arranging. Miller, who is six hours shy of a master's degree in music education, said members of E.T.C. didn't know much about music before they enrolled in the program, but they had a lot of interest. About 75 youths from 8 to 18 participate in the music program. Cost is $1.00.

Today, E.T.C. members assist with the program, and they participate in a master class with other professionals and conduct clinics for students. "You never forget where you came from" said Gary Williams. "That's where most of us developed our potential." Some members also have taken private lessons.

Gospel Background

Miller said the group has donated some of its profits to the Boys' Club and has loaned equipment to the music program. Both Gary Williams and Adolph Williams received the top honors at the Club for "Boy of the Year" for their involvement in the home, church, school, community and Boys' Club.

The musical background of E.T.C. members goes back as far as 17 years. Gary Williams, for example, said he has been singing since he was 5. He has a background in gospel music through attending New Bethel Church of God In Christ.

The other lead vocalist Roderick Jones, who sings falsetto, learned gospel music at Holy Ghost Temple. In addition, he has performed in Show Wagons sponsored by the Omaha Parks and Recreation Department and The World Herald.

The group has about 10 outfits for different performances. Those include everything from casual wear to tuxedos. One outfit includes $100.00 white cowboy boots, black slacks, white shirts and black cowboy hats. "We're very versatile, and it comes out in our uniform and our music," said Jerry Riggs.

Adolph Williams said the group has been successful because of its "ability to come together and play different styles." "It used to be a project, something to do for fun," said Gregory Bowie. "Now it's a business. We have to make sure we have things together. This is a career, our Future." Omaha World Herald, Omaha, Nebraska, May 30, 1982.[xxxv]

No one is better equipped to give more background information about this band except the late great Sibyl Myers, the group's long time manager, she writes:

Gary T. Williams, songwriter/lead vocals,
"Gary has had a hunger for music since he was five years old. That's when he began singing gospel at New Bethel Church

of God in Christ in Omaha. Since then, he has grown into an all-around performer who loves to sing, dance and act. He also has become a songwriter, intrigued by the act of sending messages through song.

Among the tunes he has composed for the E.T.C. Band are: "ET Cetra," "Hummin'," "My Friend" and "Love Ain't Nothing like It Used to Be." In addition, he has choreographed most of the intricate steps that are the trademark of the band.

As a singer, Gary is electrifying. He sings second tenor and is featured on the band's renditions of Stevie Wonder's "Ribbon in the Sky," and "If This World Were Mine" by Luther Vandross. A natural performer, Gary's sparkling personality has warmed many audiences. An Aquarius, he also plays percussion. His interests includes basketball, skiing, tennis and working with children.

Roderick Jones, lead vocals,

They call him "Sweet R.J.," a nickname he has had since he was a teen-ager. Falsetto is his style, which has sent, chills down the spines of many women in the audience. As a soloist, he shines on E.T.C.'s original "With You" and on "Open Arms" by Journey and "One Hundred Ways" by Quincy Jones featuring James Ingram.

Rod also plays keyboards, but he prefers to dazzle people with his voice. He began singing gospel music at Holy Ghost Temple in Omaha when he was about six. Since then, he has taken voice lessons to improve his natural talent.

He first got into show business by acting in community productions when he was a youngster. An Aries, Rod's favorite performer is Smokey Robinson. He also enjoys weight lifting and racing cars.

Michael B. Adams 2nd, songwriter/keyboards,

Michael's songwriting is an extension of his smooth playing style. Among the tunes he has composed for E.T.C. are two love songs, "Time on You" and "With You." He likes writing from the heart.

He also likes to let the keyboards do the talking as he often closes his eyes to the outside world as his fingers ring out the notes. Although Michael's playing style is smooth, it also is aggressive, particularly during solos on the band's originals "Hummin'" and "Et Cetera" and on "Wide Shot" by Superior Movement.

On stage, Michael plays the Fender Rhodes electric piano, Moog Opus III and Moog Prodigy. However, despite the wide variety of highly technological keyboard equipment available today, his favorite instrument remains a Steinway Grand Piano.

A Gemini, Michael's favorite style of music is jazz and his favorite performer is Chick Correa. He also enjoys anything involving motor vehicles from racing them to fixing them.

<u>*Jerry Riggs*</u>*, drums,*

Bouncing with the beat, Jerry's bold style is one you won't easily forget. He is the pacesetter of the group with his precision timing. On solo licks, he's in a class by himself on "Don't Stop" by Larry Graham and "Turn Up the Music" by Mass Production.

Jerry has had an attachment to drums since he was a youngster. He started his musical career at home with drums made out of common household items. Since then, he has become a punchy percussionist who is always ready to try something new.

His favorite music is anything with a beat—jazz, soul, pop or rock. His favorite musician is Billy Cobham. Duke answers to the nickname "Duke C.," a variation of his middle name. He is a Taurus who likes to play basketball in his free time.

<u>*Greg Bowie*</u>*, bass guitar/vocals,*

Music hit Greg when he was still in diapers. When he was about ten, he would make believe the broom was a bass and jam to a record. He got his first bass guitar and amplifier on his 12th birthday.

Now with about 10 years of experience under his belt, Greg has developed a vigorous, hard-hitting fill-in style. Unique and funky are his trademarks on solos such as E.T.C.'s original "Et

Cetera" and on "Don't Stop" by Larry Graham. Greg also sings tenor as a background vocalist. Other musical talents include playing percussion.

Greg acquired the nickname "Baby Face" through his association with E.T.C. A Gemini, his favorite music is funk. He also enjoys playing football and basketball.

Adolph Williams, trumpet/flugelhorn/vocals,

Call him Mr. Versatility. He sings, dances, writes arrangements and plays trumpet and flugelhorn. That's on-stage. Off-stage, he does electrical work for the band and handles many of the business matters.

To Adolph, music is an international language and his goal is to be the deliverer of the message to all people. His message on-stage comes through on horn solos on E.T.C.'s original song, "Time on You" and on "ICan't Get over You" by the Gap Band. Adolph has teamed with saxophone-player Charles Williams to form "The W-Horns."

Adolph first got interested in music through his participation in a local drum and bugle corps when he was a youngster. From there, he has participated in almost every type of band imaginable—pep, marching, stage and rock. In addition, he has played with an orchestra.

His favorite musicians include: Stevie Wonder, Quincy Jones and Freddy Hubbard. When he's not working with E.T.C., Adolph enjoys playing tennis, biking, and motorcycle riding and working with children. He is a Taurus.

Charles Williams, saxophone/vocals,

With the nickname of "Sax," Charles is the other half of the band's "W-Horns." He has about 10 years of experience as a saxophone player. Including three years with the U.S. Army Band stationed outside of Boston, Mass. He received advanced individualized training at the Army School of Music in Norfolk, Va., where professionals such as Doc Severinsen and Grover Washington have studied and taught.

As a member of the Army Band, Charles traveled throughout New England playing in parades and at military *ceremonies in addition to playing big band jazz. The newest member of the E.T.C. Band, his mellow style is at its best on "The One You Love" by Glenn Frey. But Charles' style is wild as well as peaceful, particularly during solos on "Big Fun" and "Get Down on It" by Kool & the Gang and on "Hard to Get" by Rick James.*

Charles assists vocally by singing second tenor. His favorite type of music is funk jazz. A Taurus, he enjoys football and weigh lifting when he is not playing with the band. Sibyl Myers, (The group's long time manager).[xxxvi]

⅃

The excitement and energy of the E.T.C. Band took the Midlands by storm. People who heard their music for the first time instantly became followers because the music of E.T.C. stayed with them long after the event was over. The group generated enthusiasm and energized their audiences.

In only a few years, E.T.C. bucked the odds and became a success at home, which usually is the hardest place for anyone to gain recognition. Most people in Omaha had a love affair for E.T.C. that words cannot describe. Their move to the 20's Night Club proved to be very rewarding. This was the most prestige club to perform at in the metro Omaha area. To play here meant you were part of the big time local scene. The group is pictured below at the 20's.

Photo courtesy of Chuck Miller

Classic E.T.C. Band at the 20's Night Club, June 26-28, 1986.

Left to right: Roderick Jones, vocals; Adolph Williams, trumpet; Jerry "Duke" Riggs, drums; Gary Williams, vocals; Charlie Williams, alto saxophone; Michael B. Adams 2nd, keyboards; and Greg Bowie, bass.

After pleasing the people at home, the group decided to take the show on the road. Here is how this came about, Gary Williams remembers:

ᄔ

<u>Gary T. Williams</u>, songwriter/lead vocals.

Photo courtesy of Michael B. Adams 2nd

E.T.C. Band Member, Gary "TeeLuv" Williams in Japan.

My older sister Verna was an Executive for the military. She ran all of the military housings. She came back home from

Hawaii and saw E.T.C. perform at the Ranch Bowl and met Sibyl Myers, the group's manager. They both collaborated and got the group the connection for a Mid West tour and the Air Force Tour of Japan.

The group then consists of Jerry "Duke" Riggs, drums, Greg Bowie, bass, Charlie Williams, tenor saxophone, Roderick Jones, vocals, Clarence Nichols, guitar, Michael B. Adams 2nd, keyboards, and me Gary Williams, vocals. Clarence had been with the group about four or five years.

Photo courtesy of Michael B. Adams 2nd

E.T.C. Band.

Left to right, row one: Gary Williams, vocals; left to right, row two: Roderick Jones, vocals; Greg Bowie, bass; Jerry "Duke" Riggs, drums; Michael B. Adams 2nd, keyboards; Clarence Nichols, guitar; Row three: Charlie Williams, tenor/alto saxophone;

Before going to Japan, the group went on a road tour to Colorado and stayed quite some times. Then we went to

Canada. We returned from Canada and went to the Grand Canyon. We next went to Oklahoma and Texas, and then returned to the Grand Canyon.

E.T.C. In Hawaii & Japan

In 1986 we went to Hawaii and later experienced our first over Seas tour through Japan. We then went to Korea, the Philippians and returned to the States and went back to Colorado and the Grand Canyon again. We then came back to Omaha and went on a band retreat. This is when Chuck Miller came in and gave us a music workshop.

Photo courtesy of Michael B. Adams 2nd

E.T.C. Band Members with the Debarge Brothers.

Left to right: Bobby Debarge; Michael B. Adams 2nd, Charlie Williams, and James Debarge.

Photo courtesy of Michael B. Adams 2nd

E.T.C. Band Member.

Greg Bowie with his fancy bass guitar.

Photo courtesy of Michael B. Adams 2nd

E.T.C. Band Members with the Temptations.

Photo courtesy of Michael B. Adams 2nd

E.T.C. Band Member.

Michael B. Adams 2nd, keyboards.

Photo courtesy of Michael B. Adams 2nd

E.T.C. Band Member in Japan.

Michael B. Adams 2nd, keyboards.

Photo courtesy of Michael B. Adams 2nd

E.T.C. Band Members with an International Group in Japan.

Photo courtesy of Michael B. Adams 2nd

E.T.C. Band Members with Herbie Hancock in Japan.

Left to right: Michael B. Adams 2nd, Herbie Hancock.

Michael Adams' uncle, Mal Adams moved to Japan to start a CNN Network for National New Coordinator, Ted Turner. Mal then started his own company called, "Country Media." When E.T.C. went through Japan on our way to Korea, Mal came to the Air Base and picked the group up and brought us into town and we played at a club called Pixel and we performed quite well. Mr. O'Hara, the owner of the Pixel said, "Yall are to live for my place, yall need to be at the Tokyo Dome."

Photo courtesy of Michael B. Adams 2nd

Mount Fuji in Japan.

We continued on with our tour and performed in Okinawa and at all of the Japan Air force Bases. We made quite a lot of money during this time. We all said that we were going to come back to Japan when the tour was over because Mal Adams had gotten us another gig at The Pink Lemon. However; some of the other band members didn't want to do the gig. They later got home sick and wanted to return home.

We returned home and hired vocalist Melony Watkins who traveled with us to Canada and almost ruined the gig. After I corrected her for her bad behavior on stage, she started crying. Adolph Williams and Jerry "Duke" Riggs tried to get me to apologize to Melony and I got in an argument with them.

Photo courtesy of Michael B. Adams 2nd

E.T.C. vocalist, Melony Watkins.

I then said, "I tell you what, after this gig is over, this will be my last time with the band." I predicted that six months after this incident, the band would be finished because I felt that the band couldn't exist without me. Believe it or not, this prediction came true. I left the band at the end of July of 1989. The group kept on playing gigs and hired Mario Corbino, Melony's brother to replace me as vocalist. Mario is pictured below with internationally recording group called Club Nouveau whom he joined after he left E.T.C. Band. Notice on the side bar the thanks he gives Chuck Miller for helping him with his success:

CLUB NOUVEAU

Photo courtesy of Mario Corbino

Club Nouveau.

Left to right: Vocalist Mario Corbino and Club Nouveau.

My prediction about the band came true; while the band was preparing to play a gig, one of the members didn't show up for the engagement and the band was fired for the first time. After that, the band called it quits.

After the band broke up, Michael went back to Japan and two years later I followed him. We both have made Japan our home as to this day. Williams, Gary, Telephone Interview with Chuck Miller, (11 Jan. 09), Tokyo, Japan.[xxxvii]

Photo courtesy of the Internet

Fred W. Schott, Current PRESIDENT & CEO, Boys and Girls Clubs of the Midlands.

This is my second time around. I worked with kids at the Omaha Clubs from 1972 – 1980. One never really leaves a lifetime passion, but I 'returned' in 2002 after a 22-year career in business. Much has changed since then and the challenges are greater than ever.

Today, we are challenging every child to reach their full potential. The challenge arises out of an enduring, never changing belief that every child is gifted in some way and it's up to all of us to uncover each one's special gifts.

Across America and our own community are thousands of alumni. Some of them are prominent leaders, most are just average people. The one thing almost all of them will tell you is that the Club made a real difference for them. Many will say, "The Club may have saved my life."

No reward or recognition compares with an adult approaching you in an airport, a store, an athletic event or other public place, smiling broadly, sticking out a hand and asking, "Remember me? I grew up at the Club." There is nothing like it. Join us in making a difference. http://www.bgcomaha.org/discover/administration.[xxxviii]

Photo courtesy of Chuck Miller

*Professor Charles L (a.k.a. Chuck Miller),
author of A Bridge to Success, 2010.*

PROFESSOR CHARLES L. MILLER, Conductor, keyboard synthesis/lead and back- up vocals and manager for many of his groups has many talents in many areas. His national professional experience includes: recording and performing with The Esquires & the Fabulous Rhinestones and The Paul Butterfield Blues Band. He has also appeared in concert with Loggins and Messina, The Dazz Band, Switch, New Edition, jazz guitarist Kenny Burrell and Grover Washington, Jr. Chuck is the first African American student to graduate from the University of Nebraska at Omaha, Music Department; a graduate of The University of Nebraska in Lincoln, Nebraska and a graduate of Rutgers University's *Mason Gross School of the Arts* in New Brunswick, New Jersey. He also attended Berklee College of

Music in Boston, Mass for a year. He is currently a Professor of Music for Music in Catholic Schools Bands and a former Adjunct Professor for the Black Studies Department at the University of Nebraska at Omaha.

I shall never forget the time when I performed on trumpet a little piece of music for my cousin (I use to call her my aunt) Lucy Mae Johnson and her husband Theodore. I was only in the six grade. We were in Prescott, Arkansas; standing under a tree. I played the music so well until they told me, "one day your music will be heard all over the world." Well, they were not to far from the truth, because of the Internet; my CD has sold in places as far as Japan. In fact my musical teachings through my students have taken me from Arkansas to Nebraska, Canada, England, Paris, Hawaii, Italy, Korea, the Philippians, and Japan.

I have been blessed to have been born in a small town as Prescott, Arkansas where musical resources were scarce but I was able to move to the big city of Omaha and influence generations of young musicians. This is what sharing is all about. These young men and women from the Gene Eppley North Omaha Boys Club (now called The Boys and Girls Clubs of the Midlands) have set a standard for excellence in music performance and have made a mark in the lives of generations that will live on in the hearts of many forever. I am so proud of all of their accomplishments.

God bless all of you,

Chuck Miller
www.sealottmusic.com

Photo courtesy of "Ain't No Stopping Us Now Documentary"

Future Musician, Branden T. Miller, 2010.

Branden T. Miller, alto saxophone, bass, keyboards and videographer.

Photo courtesy of "Ain't No Stopping Us Now Documentary"

Ain't No Stopping Us Now Documentary musicians, 2010.

<u>Left to right</u>: **Row one**: Andre Davis, Agent/D.J., Chuck Miller, trumpet, vocals, keyboards and author, Mario Corbino, vocals, bass, keyboards and recording artist, Nikita Sampson, vocals, keyboards and recording artist. Left to right: **Row two**: Mark "Bam-Bam" McKee, drums and keyboards, Terrance Bailey, guitar and vocals, Robert Smith, vocals, drums and recording artist. Left to right: **Row three**: Robert Holmes, guitar, Craig Franklin, keyboards, bass, vocals and recording artist, Thomas Wells, bass, keyboards and recording artist, David Bailey, bass and vocals and Richard Williams, bass and recording artist.

END NOTES

[i] Revelation 2:76, The Living Bible Version

[ii] Galatians 5:22-23, The Living Bible Version

[iii] http://en.wikipedia.org/wiki/Jimmy_Witherspoon (11 July 2010)

[iv] http://en.wikipedia.org/wiki/David_Ruffin (11 July 2010)

[v] Photo courtesy of UNO Year Book

[vi] UNO Tomahawk p. 55

[vii] Photo courtesy of UNO Year Book

[viii] http://en.wikipedia.org/wiki/Luigi_Waites

[ix] http://www.raremp3.co.uk/2010/06/fabulous-rhinestones-freewheelin-1973.html (12 July 2010)

[x] Eder, Bruce, All Music Guide. http://www.cmt.com/artists/az/fabulous_rhinestones/bio.jhtml (12 July 2010)

[xi] The Metro News Paper, Week of March 14, 1974.

[xii] U.N.O. Gateway News Paper, Week of October 25, 1974.

[xiii] Howell, Calvin, Telephone Interview with Chuck Miller, (11 Jan. 09), Orlando, Florida.

[xiv] Denis E. Waitley, Ph.D. (The Psychology of Winning).

[xv] Teachout, David (Can Music Education help At-Risk Students?).

[xvi] The Omaha Star, Vol. 65 – No. 12, Omaha, Nebraska, Thursday, May 15, 2003, front page.

[xvii] Howell, Calvin, Telephone Interview with Chuck Miller, (11 Jan. 09), Orlando, Florida.

[xviii] ibid

[xix] Inner City News, Week of December 1975.

[xx] Howell, Calvin, Telephone Interview with Chuck Miller, (11 Jan. 09), Orlando, Florida.

[xxi] ibid

[xxii] Lawson, Greg, Telephone Interview with Chuck Miller, (13 Jan. 09).

[xxiii] The Omaha Star, Gerald Evans.

xxiv Howell, Calvin, Telephone Interview with Chuck Miller, (11 Jan. 09), Orlando, Florida.

xxv Fisher McClinton, Bryant, Telephone Interview with Chuck Miller, (11 Jan. 09), Nebraska, Omaha.

xxvi The Omaha Black Music Hall of Fame, summer of 2007.

xxvii Ginger "Dee" Davis, Destiny's drummer.

xxviii Calloway, Jim, (Black Scene Magazine), October, 1971, Omaha, Nebraska.

xxix The Air Pulse, January 22, 1975.

xxx Grant, Eddie, (Battle of the bands at the Clouds), Telephone Interview with Chuck Miller, (13 Jan. 09), Omaha, Nebraska.

xxxi The Omaha Star, "Square Biz" Takes Omaha By Storm, Omaha, Nebraska, July 31, 1986.

xxxii http://www.steppenstonz.com/id7.html (12 July 2010).

xxxiii Photo http://www.steppenstonz.com/id8.html

xxxiv Photo http://www.steppenstonz.com/id4.html

xxxv Omaha World Herald, Omaha, Nebraska, May 30, 1982.

xxxvi Sibyl Myers, (The group's long time manager).

xxxvii Williams, Gary, Telephone Interview with Chuck Miller, (11 Jan. 09), Tokyo, Japan.

xxxviii http://www.bgcomaha.org/discover/administration